# RULES FOR RADICALS DEFEATED

JEFF HEDGPETH

a.k.a. AlinskyDefeater

ISBN: 1475192037
ISBN-13: 13: 978-1475192032

# DEDICATION

To Anna, who believes in me even when I don't believe in myself.

# CONTENTS

# DISCLAIMER

Anything contained in this book that is not documented is strictly the opinion of the author.

# 1

## *Who was Alinsky? What is Rules for Radicals, and why should I care?*

*"Victorious warriors win first and then go to war, while defeated warriors go to war first and then seek to win" — Sun Tzu, The Art of War*

## *Saul Alinsky*

The days of traditional politics are over. Conservatives would be well served to abandon the acquiescent political hand wringing, and build the skills necessary to engage and defeat their opponents. In the age of Obama, politics has morphed into one part traditional political strategy mixed with one or more parts Saul Alinsky's *Rules for Radicals*. We must find a way to defeat our opponents without becoming them. To defeat their morally bankrupt schemes it will be necessary to learn their tactics well.

Simply learning their tactics and then turning them back on them, however, will make us no better than those we oppose. Learn the tactics we must, but we must also supplement our understanding of Alinsky with morally sound principles designed specifically to defeat them. This book will provide you with an understanding of Alinsky's tactics, and morally sound principles to oppose them.

The name Saul Alinsky seems to have been resurrected from obscurity in the past few years. He was a community organizer whose work ranged from the 1930's to the 1970's, and was most famous for his book *Rules for Radicals*, wherein he outlined a set of tactics for revolution. His goal was to empower the "Have-nots" in such a way that they could overpower the "Haves", and create a new, fairer society. If it sounds a lot like Marxism to you, well, you're not alone. Although his book has remained somewhat popular over the years, it was the emergence of Barack Obama on the national political scene that truly brought Alinsky back into the limelight; and even though he died in 1972, *Rules for Radicals* became the Bible for community organizers like Barack Obama. As you will see, the tactics taught in that book are both ruthless and effective.

When I first joined twitter in July of 2009 under the name *AlinskyDefeater*, it was still quite common for people to ask me what my name meant. As you can imagine, I'm rarely asked that question these days. Before Barack Obama ran for President, few had heard the name Saul Alinsky or heard of his most famous book, *Rules for Radicals*. The name Saul Alinsky is not such a mystery these days. While many on both sides of the political aisle had never heard of Saul Alinsky before Barack Obama began running for President, there were the devoted few who were quite aware of Alinsky and his tactics well before that time. Many of us first learned of Alinsky during the Presidency of Bill Clinton. After all, Hillary had written her senior thesis at Wellesley on The Alinsky Model. Subsequently, she had been offered a job working for Alinsky, a job she turned down. I have supplied references at the back of the book, but if you're looking for Hillary's thesis it was entitled, *"THERE IS ONLY THE FIGHT..."- An Analysis of the Alinsky Model.*[1]

So just who was this Saul Alinsky, and why is he still so revered in Leftist circles? I will keep my biographical sketch of Alinsky extremely brief, because it is not the man I wish to counter in this book, but his ideas.

Saul David Alinsky (January 30, 1909 – June 12, 1972) is commonly referred to as the Father of Community Organizing. As David Horowitz says,

> His preferred self-description was "rebel" and his entire life was devoted to organizing a revolution in America to destroy a system he regarded as oppressive and unjust. By profession, he was a "community organizer," the same term employed by his most famous disciple, Barack Obama, to describe himself. [2]

Alinsky's early career was that of a criminal sociologist. His biographer, Sanford Horwitt paints a picture of a man working for a prison system, but more attuned to the plight of the inmates than to a law abiding society. He found a kinship with the inmates, and he found himself blaming society for their "misfortune" rather than blaming the individuals for their own behavior. This philosophy would permeate the rest of Alinsky's life's work. He always viewed the problems of poverty and

3

crime through the prism of what society had done to the criminal, rather than what the criminal had done to his victim.[3]

Becoming bored with his work as a sociologist, Alinsky eventually moved on to work in the Back of the Yards in Chicago, an extremely poor, heavily immigrant area made famous in Upton Sinclair's famous book *The Jungle*. It was in this tough atmosphere that Alinsky cut his teeth as a community organizer, and formed many of the principles for community organization that would make up his first book *Reveille for Radicals*, the predecessor to his more famous work, *Rules for Radicals*.

*Rules for Radicals* was written as a guidebook for radicals. It embodies general principles by which revolution can be accomplished. Just what that revolutions' end was to be is never defined by Alinsky. He describes his work by saying,

> In this book I propose certain general observations, propositions, and concepts of the mechanics of mass movements and the various stages of the cycle of action and reaction in revolution. [4]

And again,

> Here I propose to present an arrangement of certain facts and general concepts of change, a step forward toward a science of revolution.[5]

It is this same general approach, against which I intend to defend. I will not offer specifics anymore than Alinsky did, but rather general principles by which Conservatives can defend themselves against these insidious and unscrupulous tactics. To my knowledge, no one has yet set forth such a generalized defense against Alinsky tactics.

## *Community Organizing and Rules for Radicals*

When Barack Obama burst on the scene in 2007, the term "Community Organizer" was thrust to the forefront of the national dialogue. Unfortunately, in the interim, far too few have taken the time to discover exactly what community organizing is, and just how influential the tactics of Saul Alinsky have become in American politics. As Thomas Jefferson said,

> "Whenever the people are well-informed, they can be trusted with their own government; that whenever things get so far wrong as to attract their notice, they may be relied on to set them to rights."[6]

*Rules for Radicals* is looked upon as the Bible of the Leftist revolution and counterculture. It contains principles designed to help the would-be radical foment a revolution – a revolution that is intended to bring down capitalism, and usher in a new age of utopian bliss. While these goals are the boilerplate hippie, pie in the sky stuff we're all accustomed to, the tactics themselves are quite ingenious. They offer overarching principles that radicals can use to defeat their enemies. These tactics are the very same tactics used by Hillary Clinton, and, more successfully, by Barack Obama and his team of advisors. The astonishing part is that the Right always seems surprised when they are attacked with Alinsky tactics, and instead of formulating a reasonable defense, they simply complain that the other side is using unfair tactics. I hope this book can go a long way in rectifying that situation.

So why are we suddenly hearing more and more about this seemingly obscure and rather out-dated community organizer? Many on the Left would have us believe that the name Saul Alinsky is some sort of Right-wing boogeyman, and that those who mention him in relation to Barack Obama are nothing more than alarmists or racists seeking to besmirch the President. The Right, to its credit, has grown increasingly aware of Saul Alinsky and *Rules for Radicals*. A close examination of Obama and the people he surrounds himself with reveals a group of politicians who rely almost exclusively on the tactics explained in *Rules for Radicals*. When you understand those tactics, it paints a picture of the way in which Obama and his people operate, and it's not a pretty picture. Alinsky tactics are ruthless even by the standards of modern day American politics. As I said, the Left, does its part to make us believe that the Alinsky-Obama connection is a fabrication of, as Hillary Clinton once famously said, "a vast Right-wing conspiracy". In the pages that follow, I will demonstrate the Alinsky-Obama connection, just why the Alinsky model is such a dangerous one, and how we, as ordinary citizens, can fight back against this pernicious, anti-American philosophy. In a recent Republican debate, Newt Gingrich said,

> "Those two choices, I believe, will give the American people a chance to decide permanently whether we want to remain the historic America that has provided opportunity for more people of more backgrounds than any country in history, or whether, in fact, we prefer to become a brand-new, secular, European-style, bureaucratic socialist system.

> The America of the Declaration of Independence v. the America of Saul Alinsky; the America of paychecks v. the America of food stamps; the America of Independence v. the America of Dependence; the America of strength in foreign policy v. the America of weakness in foreign policy."[7]

Suddenly the subject of Saul Alinsky had become no longer merely the fodder of Conservative radio talk shows or Fox News opinion shows like Sean Hannity. Now, Alinsky and his tactics had found their way, about four years too late I might add, front and center in American Presidential Politics. The Left, however, still seeks to cloister Alinsky as though his tactics are either quaint and innocent or simply not relevant. A recent Huffington Post article (January 2012) was entitled, *Saul Alinsky: "A GOP Bogeyman Who Influences Many On The Left And Right"* In that article, the author, Luke Johnson, attempts to both paint Alinsky as an innocuous figure, and simultaneously distance Barack Obama from Alinsky's teachings. He quotes from an article by Ryan Lizza,

> "However, although Obama didn't quite find himself reliving the civil rights era, he soon found himself succumbing to the appeal of Alinsky's organizing methodology.
>
> In *Dreams*, Obama spent some 150 pages on his four years in Chicago working as an organizer, but there's little discussion of the theory that undergirded his work and informed that of his teachers. Alinsky is the missing layer of his account."[8]

He goes on to say Obama has been critical of Alinsky. Specifically, he quotes Obama as saying,

7

> "It's true that the notion of self-interest was critical," said Obama to Lizza. "But Alinsky understated the degree to which people's hopes and dreams and their ideals and their values were just as important in organizing as people's self-interest."

This quote makes Obama sound somehow idealistic rather than ideological. It paints him as selfless and compassionate, a man simply seeking to help his fellow man find his way. What Johnson fails to quote from that article by Lizza is the following,

> "Not long after Obama arrived, he sat down for a cup of coffee in Hyde Park with a fellow organizer named Mike Kruglik. Obama's work focused on helping poor blacks on Chicago's South Side fight the city for things like job banks and asbestos removal. His teachers were schooled in a style of organizing devised by Saul Alinsky, the radical University of Chicago-trained social scientist. At the heart of the Alinsky method is the concept of "agitation"-- making someone angry enough about the rotten state of his life that he agrees to take action to change it; or, as Alinsky himself described the job, to "rub raw the sores of discontent."[9]

Such convenient editing (even of his own material) is common on both sides of the political spectrum, and it is wrong no matter which side is engaging in such scurrilous behavior. That point aside, these 2007 articles already painted the picture of a young Barack Obama who bought into Saul Alinsky's amoral tactics. We see a young Obama bent on change, change defined as good only in the minds of those doing the changing, and change that gave no thought to the morality of the means by which it was actuated. Soon this "Hope and Change" candidate would have audiences swooning with his soaring rhetoric, but it is doubtful that those throngs of admirers truly understood just what type of "change" Barack Obama had in mind. Could they possibly have understood what he meant when he declared prior to the 2008 Presidential election, "In five days we are going to fundamentally transform America"?[10]

Little did people know that Obama was lifting his "Hope and Change" campaign straight from the pages of his leftist, counterculture guidebook. In *Rules for Radicals*, Alinsky says,

> "The organizer's job is to inseminate an invitation for himself, to agitate, introduce ideas, **get people pregnant with hope and a desire for change** and to identify you as the person most qualified for this purpose."[11]
> [Emphasis added]

In fact, *Rules for Radicals* is riddled with comments about hope and change. The idea of change is the central theme of the book, but the type of change Alinsky envisioned is probably not the type of change Americans were seeking in 2008. The country was war-weary, and in the midst of a financial crisis, the likes of which it had not seen for 50 years. Hope, to Obama's adoring throngs meant jobs, a solid financial sector, a graceful way out of the wars in Afghanistan and Iraq, and much more, but it is almost certain that those listening to Obama in 2008 never thought that change meant all-out class warfare. However, it is class warfare in the style of Karl Marx that litters the pages of Alinsky's book, and it is Alinsky's book that served as the manual for the Obama campaign staff.

The Left would have you believe that any adherence by the President or his staff to Alinsky's Rules for Radicals is the product of the fevered imaginations of paranoid Right-wingers. So, let us examine the connection between Obama and Alinsky, and whether that connection is a cause for concern.

## *The Obama – Alinsky Connection*

When White House spokesperson Jay Carney was asked recently whether there was anything to President Obama's ties to Saul Alinsky, his response was far from an absolute denial. Instead, Mr. Carney said,

> "The President's background as a community organizer is well documented in the President's own books. So, his experience in that field obviously contributed to ...um ... who he is today. But his experience is a broad-based one and includes a lot of other areas of ...uh...in his life. So, I'll just leave it at that."[12]

Now, does that sound like the White House itself is running from its relationship with Alinsky, and Alinsky tactics? Ed Henry, the White House correspondent who proffered that question even gave Mr. Carney the opportunity to label all the Alinsky talk as "just B.S." It is interesting that not only did Mr. Carney not avail himself of that opportunity to put daylight between the President and Saul Alinsky, but instead actually pointed out that President Obama's past experience as a community organizer is documented in Mr. Obama's books.

From his earliest days working as a community organizer in Chicago, Obama had sought to follow in the footsteps of Saul Alinsky. To a young Barack Obama, Alinsky, the father of community organizing, provided a model for creating the kind of quasi-Marxist change that both men envisioned. In his book *Dreams from My Father*, Obama makes a number of troubling statements, but for now let us consider this quote,

> "To avoid being mistaken for a white sellout, I chose my friends carefully. The more politically active black students. The foreign students. The Chicanos. The Marxist professors and structural feminists and punk-rock performance poets. We smoked cigarettes and wore leather jackets. At night, in the dorms, we discussed neocolonialism, Franz Fanon, Eurocentrism, and patriarchy."[13]

So then, Barack Obama sought out Marxist professors. While Saul Alinsky never self-identified as a Marxist, one cannot read *Rules for Radicals* without being overwhelmed by the Marxist language in which it is couched, and the entire book is a guide for radicals seeking to engage in class warfare. Is it any wonder that our President, to this day, seeks to immerse the country in this divisive class warfare as a political strategy for his own gain?

A recent article in Investors.com outlines several of the clear ties between Barak Obama and the father of community organizers, Saul Alinsky. The author of the editorial points out the following ties:

- In 1988, Obama even wrote a chapter for the book "After Alinsky: Community Organizing in Illinois," in which he lamented organizers' "lack of power" in implementing change.

- Gamaliel board member John McKnight, a hard-core student of Alinsky, penned a letter for Obama to help him get into Harvard Law School.

- Obama took a break from his Harvard studies to travel to Los Angeles for eight days of intense training at Alinsky's Industrial Areas Foundation, a station of the cross for acolytes.

- In turn, he trained other community organizers in Alinsky agitation tactics.

- Obama also taught Alinsky's "Power Analysis" methods at the University of Chicago.

- During the presidential campaign, Obama hired one of his Gamaliel mentors, Mike Kruglik, to train young campaign workers in Alinsky tactics at "Camp Obama," a school set up at Obama headquarters in Chicago. The tactics helped Obama capture the youth vote like no other president before him.

- Power would no longer be an issue, as Obama infiltrated the highest echelon of the political establishment — the White House — fulfilling Alinsky's vision of a new "vanguard" of coat-and-tie radicals who "work inside the system" to change the system.

- After the election, his other Gamaliel mentor, Jerry Kellman (who hired him and whose identity Obama disguised in his memoir), helped the Obama administration establish Organizing for America, which mobilizes young supporters to agitate for Obama's legislative agenda using "Rules for Radicals."[14]

I wish to leave no doubt in the reader's mind whether the ties that bind Alinsky and Obama are real or imagined. Indeed Barack and Michelle Obama's first meeting was infused with the memory and adoration of Saul Alinsky. Michelle Obama, addressing the 2008 Democratic National Convention, had these words about the first time that she met a young Barack Obama,

> "And Barack stood up that day, and he spoke words that have stayed with me ever since. He talked about the world as it is, and the world as it should be. And he said that all too often we accept the distance between the two, and we settle for the world as it is even when it doesn't reflect our values and aspirations."[15]

Meanwhile, the very first sentence of the very first chapter of Saul Alinsky's Rules for Radicals reads,

> "What follows is for those who want to change the world from what it is to what they believe is should be."[16]

And on page 12 Alinsky continues,

> "The basic requirement for the understanding of the politics of change is to recognize the world as it is. We must work with it on its

terms if we are to change it to the kind of world we would like it to be. We must see the world as it is and not as we would like it to be."[17]

Any student of Alinsky could not miss the message. It is the premise of *Rules for Radicals*. So then, at their very first meeting, Barack and Michelle Obama united over the words of Saul Alinsky, and it was Alinsky's words that weaved the backdrop to their first intellectual and romantic connection; troubling and a bit creepy.

The connection between Alinsky and Obama is not only dangerous, but the Alinsky influence is so pervasive in this President that it appears that it is difficult for him to think outside of this paradigm. Every reaction comes, not from some manufactured sense of what Alinsky's tactics might tell him to do, but from a man so saturated in Alinsky's teachings that no thought is necessary. Obama is so versed, so well trained in Alinsky tactics, that where Alinsky's teachings stop and Obama's thoughts begin is, at times, almost imperceptible. After all, Obama not only learned Alinsky's tactics, he actually taught them.[18]

If all of this was not enough to convince you of the link between Saul Alinsky and Barack Obama, perhaps the words of Saul Alinsky's son, writing for the Boston Globe, might convince you:

# *Son sees father's handiwork in convention*

August 31, 2008

ALL THE elements were present: the individual stories told by real people of their situations and hardships, the packed-to-the-rafters crowd, the crowd's chanting of key phrases and names, the action on the spot of texting and phoning to show instant support and commitment to jump into the political battle, the rallying selections of music, the setting of the agenda by the power people. The Democratic National Convention had all the elements of the perfectly organized event, Saul Alinsky style.

Barack Obama's training in Chicago by the great community organizers is showing its effectiveness. It is an amazingly powerful format, and the method of my late father always works to get the message out and get the supporters on board. When executed meticulously and thoughtfully, it is a powerful strategy for initiating change and making it really happen. Obama learned his lesson well.

I am proud to see that my father's model for organizing is being applied successfully beyond local community organizing to affect the Democratic campaign in 2008. It is a fine tribute to Saul Alinsky as we approach his 100th birthday.

L. DAVID ALINSKY[19]

# *Why the Alinsky-Obama Connection Matters*

Many of the goals of the far Left, and even of Alinsky, are laudable. No one on the Right is immune to the plight of the downtrodden in society. We all agree that we should be making every effort to make society better for everyone, and not a select group. The problems tend to arise when we discuss the best ways to accomplish these noble ambitions. While the Left believes that Government should take care of people, the Right believes that Government should empower people to take care of themselves. Within these two differing schools of thought, there is room for honest, intellectual discussion over the best approach, but beyond these schools of thought is a more radical view. Not all of our goals are the same. Some seek to overturn American society to build a new, "more equitable" nation on its ashes. That view is the one promoted by Alinsky. In comparing his proposed revolution to that of the American Revolution, Alinsky says,

> "The Revolution was affected before the war commenced," John Adams wrote. "The Revolution was in the hearts and minds of the people...This radical change in the principles, opinions, sentiments and affections of the people were the real American Revolution." A revolution without a prior reformation would collapse or become a totalitarian tyranny.

> A reformation means that masses of our people have reached the point of disillusionment with past ways and values. They don't know what will work but they do know that the prevailing system is self-

defeating, frustrating, and hopeless. They won't act for change but won't strongly oppose those who do. The time is then ripe for revolution."[20]

Alinsky is calling for a revolution as stark, and as real as the American Revolution. He is saying that society has reached a tipping point where a group of trained radicals can lead a new revolution, and those who won't help will at least not oppose.

The entire chapter entitled, "The Purpose" is essentially a treatise for the tenets of Marxism, and the need for a revolution against the power establishment. While Alinsky is careful never to self-identify for fear of losing the support of opposing groups, his ideas and even his language is clearly Marxist. It is clear that Alinsky endorses Marxism – you know the same kind of Marxism taught by those professors that Barack Obama sought out. While the book is replete with Marxist phrases and ideas, let me offer just one quote to show the flavor of Alinsky's Marxist ideology,

> "The setting for the drama of change has never varied. Mankind has been and is divided into three parts: the Haves, the Have-Nots, and the Have-a-Little, Want Mores.
>
> On top are the Haves with power, money, food, security, and luxury. They suffocate in their surpases while the Have-Nots starve. Numerically the Haves have always been the fewest. The Haves want to keep things as they are and are opposed to change. Thermopolitically they are cold and determined to freeze the status quo."[21]

While no one is claiming that American society is perfect, the ultimate war that rages below the surface of the Obama/Alinsky model, and traditional American thought is the war between collectivism and individualism. It is a war between the Alinsky/Marx view where America and its capitalistic society play the part of villain, and a more traditional American belief system founded on the Declaration of Independence and the Constitution of the United States. A belief system where America is the protagonist defending a system of bottom up governance against attempts by Alinsky and others to create a top down system of governance.

Perhaps a tendency towards some sort of socialist or quasi-Marxist view was natural in light of the complete meltdown of the financial sector in 2008. Since the time of Karl Marx, and his conclusion that Capitalism must necessarily end in Marxist revolt, and ultimately in the "paradise" of Communism, there has been a rather natural tendency of people to look to Marxism and Communism when it appears Capitalism has apparently failed. This explains the rise of Marxism and Communism during the depression, and it helps to define why America would elect Barack Obama after the crash of 2008.

While such a tendency may, in some ways, seem natural it does not make it correct. Capitalism has corrected itself before, and will do so again. The real problem is not with free enterprise, but with crony capitalism. Let's be clear. The real argument before us in the politics of the Left and the Right in America today is whether or not we believe that society owes it to individuals to provide a certain minimum lifestyle, or whether individuals are responsible not only for their own lot in life, but also for governing themselves. The Left espouses a Marxist model in which capitalism must be destroyed so that government can provide a level of equality for everyone. Conservatives, meanwhile, believe that capitalism must be fairly regulated so that everyone is afforded, not some governmental, a priori equality, but instead an equal opportunity. Government should provide a fair playing field, but the players should decide the game.

The choice we face here is both a political one, and a moral one. We must decide whether we choose to put our lot with the framers who declared,

> "We hold these truths to be self-evident, that all men are created equal, that they are endowed by their Creator with certain unalienable Rights, that among these are Life, Liberty and the pursuit of Happiness."[22]

Alternatively, would we rather place our trust in the likes of Marx, Engels, and Alinsky who believed that it was the responsibility of society to make certain that all men share equally in the fruits of the labor, even if they do not participate in the labor itself? Do we trust these great freedoms to the people, or do we deem the people to have acted unfairly in allowing some to have less than others, and so seek to right that wrong with the all-powerful hand of the Government?

You will have to decide which America you hold to be true – which America we shall aspire to be. Whether it be as Ronald Reagan said in his farewell address to the nation,

> "I've spoken of the Shining City all my political life. ...In my mind it was a tall, proud city built on rocks stronger than oceans, windswept, God-blessed, and teeming with people of all

kinds living in harmony and peace; a city with free ports that hummed with commerce and creativity. And if there had to be city walls, the walls had doors and the doors were open to anyone with the will and the heart to get here. That's how I saw it, and see it still."[23]

Or whether you would side with President Obama when he said in answer to whether he believed in American Exceptionalism or not,

"I believe in American exceptionalism, just as I suspect that the Brits believe in British exceptionalism and the Greeks believe in Greek exceptionalism."[24]

There is a wide gap between these disparate visions of America, and as you read this book, I ask you to search the innermost recesses of your mind and soul to find in which America you believe, and to find within yourself what you believe should be the noblest aspirations of the American people.

It is often methodology more than substance that separates the Alinsky model from the vision Conservatives have for America. Often, their goals start out the same, but the willingness by Alinskyites to create the envisioned change "at all cost" or "by any means necessary" causes an inevitable separation between the Alinskyite and the Conservative. The Constitution limits the methodology of the Conservative, but to the "enlightened Liberal", change for their preconceived idea of "better" is the ultimate guide, and if the Constitution stand in the way, then it is the Constitution that should change, and not their methods.

I do not seek to lay all of America's ills at the feet of Mr. Alinsky or President Obama, and I do not worship men as saints, and so no one man can fairly be said to embody all that is good about America. However, we must continually ask of our leaders that they guide us to higher, not lower, ground. We must insist that they seek to bring out the noblest intentions of mankind, and not to speak to our baser natures and encourage the very worst we have to offer. We must insist that these politicians do not feed on the desperation of the few, or upon our baser instincts.

This book is not intended as an intellectual defense of capitalism, nor is it intended as an intellectual rebuttal of Marxism. Instead it is intended as a practical text. It is intended to provide for those who are busy working, and have neither the time nor the desire to navigate the labyrinth of political views expressed through the ages. Instead, this book is intended as a practical guide to Americans who value their way of life and their God-given freedoms. It is intended as a guide to help you fight against a pernicious form of anti-American thought that has become far too prevalent in our system of politics. This book is intended to help you to understand who Saul Alinsky was, why his philosophy is dangerous, and how he has influenced our President. It is further intended to show you the methods that are being used to subvert our way of life, and how to fight back against these methods. I hope that this book will also serve as a guidebook for candidates who are besieged by Alinsky tactics. I hope that the general principles I offer to counter the Alinsky model can be of some help for honest candidates who find themselves in the maelstrom of Alinsky attacks without the slightest idea of how to defend themselves.

Once you understand who Alinsky was, and what he stood for you will begin to see how important it is that we have a way to defend against his tactics. Until recently, those who would subvert America's way of life have operated in near darkness. Too few have seen the methods they use or the intentions they harbor. Only now are we beginning to see these decades-old methods of radical subversion come to light. Unfortunately, they have come to light only after a practitioner of these methods has won the White House. You cannot defeat an enemy you cannot see, and until now they have remained hidden. They no longer operate in secret. We are onto their ways. Now, it is the job of every patriotic American to do a little studying, and become educated in the ways of Alinsky. By so doing, you will see right through the façade that is being used to subvert the traditional American way of life. Your eyes will be opened to the Marxist plan that is unfolding before us. The tactics they are using are those of a 1960's radical named Saul Alinsky. These tactics were used effectively during the 2008 Presidential campaign, they have been used by Barack Obama as President, and they will be used in the 2012 Presidential election. This time however, you will be ready. You will see through their tactics, and you will be prepared to fight back. America cannot sustain four more years of Barack Obama, and it falls upon you to fight the good fight, to expose his tactics, and to arm yourself to do battle against these insidious tactics.

What I provide here is a practical handbook for understanding and defeating Alinsky tactics. Read it. Learn it. Use it. Take the battle to them. Take America back.

## 2

# *To use or not to use – the morality of Alinsky tactics*

*The most effective means are whatever will achieve the desired results. ~Saul Alinsky*

## *Means, Ends, and Morality*

The greatest conflict for Alinsky was how to sell Liberals on the idea that they should seek to create a Utopian world, and that they should use every underhanded and devious means at their disposal to do so. How can you realistically reconcile some version of the world where we all live in John Lennon's song "Imagine", but the only way to achieve that world is by lying, cheating, and deceiving? This creates quite a dilemma – a paradox which Alinsky never satisfactorily resolves. Instead, he pilfers from

Trotsky, and does so in a rather sophomoric way. He offers no original thoughts for his self-described superior ends as justification for his reprehensible means. His argument for ends justifying means falls flat, and if this argument falls flat, his entire thesis falls with it. To seek social justice by deception and destruction seems absurd on the face of it, and yet with his paper thin arguments Alinsky has successfully duped a generation of would-be revolutionaries who seek a better world, but fail to understand the simplest concepts of right and wrong.

Nevertheless, where his intellectual justifications fall short, his methods prove quite formidable, especially when used against Conservatives who, by their very nature, seek the best in their fellow man. It is no wonder that Alinsky offers homage to Lucifer in the dedication of *Rules for Radicals*, for like Lucifer, he seeks to destroy the unsuspecting with both explicit evil, as well as by "transforming himself into an angel of light". Like Satan himself, Alinsky will use whatever means necessary to win the war. If he has to trample the naïve and the innocent under foot in the process, then they are simply the casualties of war, and Alinsky is convinced his war is just.

With the use of such ruthless tactics, how can we beat them without becoming them? The Alinsky tactics create a quandary for Conservatives, particularly those who look to their faith for a sense of morality. To many on the Right, their standards of morality will conflict with some or all of the Alinsky tactics. Nevertheless, the tactics are effective, and result in the election of people who will then be empowered to make decisions that are likely to influence the moral direction of the nation. Therefore, either way, Conservatives seem to be compelled to make some sort of moral sacrifice for the greater good. This is exactly the type of conundrum that Alinsky would enjoy. The idea that you would have to make a moral decision based upon accepting one evil to avoid another is exactly the type of notion that Alinsky would use to support his moral argument for his "at any cost" philosophy of revolution. However, do Conservatives really have to make such a choice? I would argue that they do not. Instead, we can find a way to defend against the tactics and to use the tactics only when necessary and only to the extent to which they do not betray our sense of morality. I will also present twenty principles that can be used to defeat the tactics without moral capitulation.

In the words of Alinsky's biographer,

> Alinsky would not hesitate to use anything at his disposal, and the ends definitely justified the means. He used a community center in the BYNC [Back of the Yards Neighborhood Council] where children being fed as a way as a way to both hold power over the people. And to position himself to be on the side on the needy and downtrodden.[1]

Alinsky found himself arguing with those in his own movement. Many believed it was a good idea to march and demonstrate but felt that other means were inappropriate. You'll recall that "any means necessary" was a common war cry during the sixties, and there were those who sought more militant means to stop the war in Vietnam and usher in an era of free love and peace. Not unlike prevailing thought within the counterculture of the 1960's, the Occupy Wall Street crowd of today would do well to heed the words of Alinsky when he said,

> Throughout American history every issue
> involving power and it's [sic] use has always
> carried in its wake the Liberal back wash of
> agreeing with the objective but disagreeing
> with the tactics.[2]

In defense of his "ends justify the means" approach, Alinsky presents a rather convoluted argument for the seeming lack of morality in his methodology. He borrows from differing and often conflicting philosophies and sources of morality and ethics. He is quite comfortable quoting from conflicting sources. He found it without contradiction to quote Thomas Paine, and simultaneously give an "over-the-shoulder acknowledgement" to Lucifer in the dedication of *Rules for Radicals*. He quotes from Mao and Benjamin Franklin with equal ease.

The mere mention of the word philosophy will have the eyes of many readers glassing over so I will make every attempt to avoid a more traditional exegesis of the ethical philosophy of Alinsky methods, and stick to a more practical explanation. I will not sacrifice the correctness of the solutions for the sake of simplicity. I am not "dumbing down" the moral considerations nor am I avoiding the more difficult points. I am making every attempt to keep things both accurate and practical. For those who wish to pursue a more in depth study of the moral philosophy involved in our discussion, the terms "moral dualism", "relativism", "actual consequentialism", "deontology", and "Kantianism" should give you a good start in the right direction.

Of terms mentioned above, I would like to single out consequentialism because it so clearly defines Alinsky's main school of thought as pertains to his philosophy of ethics. Technically, we would classify Alinsky's philosophy of ethics concerning his proposed methodology for change and revolution as Actual Consequentialism, which is a branch of classical Utilitarianism. Consequentialism is defined as,

> Consequentialism is a theory that asserts that normative properties only depend on the consequences. For example, the moral rightness or wrongness of an act depends on the consequences of that act, or the justice or injustice of an act depends on the consequences of that act.

And the definition of Actual Consequentialism states,

> ...that an act is morally right depends only on the actual consequences of that act, rather than any foreseeable, intended or expected consequences.[3]

In other words, the end justifies the means. Alinsky devotes an entire chapter to means and ends in his book *Rules for Radicals*. Why would he devote so much time to a philosophical discussion? The answer is simple. In order to lead his readers down a pathway that appears to be fraught with ethical conflicts, and lacking moral direction, he must first convince them that he has an answer to the obvious questions that will arise. He knew that it was outside of the norm for most people to turn to ridicule as a legitimate way to argue a moral cause. Likewise, he knew that most people would find it objectionable to target a single individual, and systematically dismantle his or her entire life in order to tie them to an opposing organization or train of thought in order to defeat it. In the same manner, many of Alinsky's tactics hinge upon the notion that the end justifies the means, and so Alinsky must establish the legitimacy of this Consequentialism as the moral basis for his proposed methods.

# *Alinsky's Argument that the End Justifies the Means*

Alinsky begins his discussion of means and ends by saying,

> That perennial Question. "Does the end justify the means?" is meaningless as it stands; the real and only question regarding the ethics of means and ends is, and always has been, "Does this particular end justify this particular means?"[4]

He then proceeds to call anyone concerned about the morality of the means involved "moralists or non-doers". He claims that virtually no one who is concerned with the morality of means has made a case rooted in reality. He claims that people who are "doing" don't have the luxury of waiting around to consider the morality of the means they employ. He compares anyone interested in the morality of means with those who allowed Hitler to come to power. Really surprised to hear the opposition compared to Hitler or complicit in his rise to power now aren't you?

Before stating his rules of the ethics of means and ends, he says of those concerned with the morality of means,

> Their fears of action drive them to refuge in and ethics so divorced from the politics of life that it can apply only to angels, not to men. The standards of judgment must be rooted in

> the whys and wherefores of life as it is lived,
> the world as it is, not our wished-for fantasy
> of the world as it should be.[5]

I find it interesting that Alinsky, while saying that the community organizer must begin with the world as it is, also opens his book by saying,

> What follows is for those who want to change
> the world from what it is to what they believe
> it should be.[6]

While his overarching goal is to provide a handbook for those who want to make the world better, he decides that when it comes to the matter of morality and ethics of means he will simply disregard any notion of improving the world. After all, if the object is to make the world better, wouldn't we want to endeavor to bring out the best in mankind concerning the ethics of means and ends? Does the noble ambition only apply as we see fit? I think the answer to that question is that noble ambition to Alinsky only applies as Alinsky sees fit. The only thing consistent about Alinsky is his inconsistencies.

Before I discuss Alinsky's eleven rules of the ethics of means, let's back up to Alinsky's chapter preceding his chapter on means and ends. In the chapter entitled, "The Purpose" he presents a window into some of the conflicting philosophies to which he subscribes. As you will see by the end of this chapter, we may consider his views inconsistent, but he simply would have argued that inconsistency is the nature of man, and so to be otherwise would be impossible. He presents a kind of moral dualism blended with Marxism and moral relativism. It's a nice blend from his perspective, because it allows him to pick and choose philosophies and morality to suit his fancy without being subject to the scrutiny a more intellectual treatise would require.

He stresses moral dualism as a backdrop for his treatment of the ethics of means. He says,

> Everything about us must be seen as the indivisible partner of its converse, light and darkness, good and evil, life and death. From the moment we are born we begin to die. Happiness and misery are inseparable. So energy conversely carries the opportunity of peace and plenty, and so with every component of this universe; all is paired in this enormous Noah's Ark of life.[7]

He goes on to say,

> This view of nature recognizes that reality is dual. The principles of Quantum mechanics in physics apply even more dramatically to the mechanics of mass movements. This is true not only in "complementarity" but in the repudiation of the hitherto universal concept of causality, whereby one always produced the other. In quantum mechanics, causality was largely replaced by probability: an electron or atom did not have to do anything specific in response to a particular force; there was just a set of probabilities that it would react in this or that way. This is fundamental in the observations and propositions which follow. At no time in any discussion or analysis of mass movements, tactics, or any other phase of the problem, can it be said that if this is done then that will result. The most we can hope to achieve is an

> understanding of the probabilities consequent to certain actions.

> This grasp of the duality of all phenomena is vital in our understanding of politics. It frees one from the myth that one approach is positive and another negative. There is no such thing in life. One man's positive is another man's negative. The description of any procedure as "positive" or "negative" is the mark of a political illiterate.[8]

I chose to quote this section at length because it speaks volumes of Alinsky's mindset. It truly does offer a window into his twisted world of morality and ethics. He claims that ethics are like quantum physics in that there is no absolute, no predictable outcome in any given situation. Instead, there is only a set of probabilities that exist, and in any given circumstances, with any corresponding given variables acting upon those circumstances, the best we can hope to predict is some set of possibilities and not a specific outcome. He bases all of this on his belief in moral relativism, which is defined as,

> Moral dualism is the belief of the great complement or conflict between the benevolent and the malignant.

> Like ditheism/bitheism (see below), moral dualism does not imply the absence of monist or monotheistic principles. Moral dualism simply implies that there are two moral opposites at work, independent of any interpretation of what might be "moral" and - unlike ditheism/bitheism - independent of how these may be represented.[9]

Alinsky needs moral dualism. He cannot present his tactics otherwise. If he is to present his tactics as the methodology for bringing about a necessary revolution of the Have-nots against the Haves, then he must remove any necessity for any moral and ethical underpinnings. After all, he is presenting rules to help community organizers transform the world from what it is to what it should be. He knows that the tactics he promulgates cannot be supported by any consistent moral framework of ethics for this purpose, because he is offering tactics that he knows are immoral as a means to accomplish a task of moral necessity. He is indignant about the moral wrong of poverty and a class-type structure in America. His *Rules for Radicals* are a set of rules useful for bringing power to that underclass. He simply cannot present the need for a moral revolution concerning class while accomplishing it through morally inconsistent means without somehow explaining (or explaining away) why poverty is a moral imperative, while the means necessary to overcome that poverty must be morally objectionable.

Alinsky is at least smart enough to know he is caught in an inconsistency. This is why he goes so far as to say that his argument for moral dualism is "fundamental in the observations and propositions which follow". We can only explain such inconsistencies if it the nature of things to be inconsistent. To understand Alinsky and his tactics we must understand that he embraces the inconsistencies. He does not shy away from them. To Alinsky, the fact that good and evil coexist in every human being is sufficient to explain such inconsistencies. Most of us would argue that while there is a duality to man, there are certain absolutes. While, at times, killing may be justified, murder is not, for example.

Inherent in this dualistic view is the understanding that the revolution he is seeking is dualistic as well. He says,

Once the nature of revolution is understood from the dualistic outlook we lose our mono-view of a revolution and see it coupled with its inevitable counterrevolution. Once we accept and learn to anticipate the inevitable counterrevolution, we may then alter the historical pattern of revolution and counterrevolution from the traditional slow advance of two steps forward and one step backward to minimizing the latter. Each element with its positive and converse sides is fused to other related elements in an endless series of everything, so that the converse of revolution on one side is counterrevolution, and on the other side, reformation, and so on in an endless chain of connected converses.[10]

We will see more about Alinsky's use of the positive and the negative when we discuss the thirteen tactics in the next chapter, but it is important to take note here that Alinsky sees the idea of a constant battle of back and forth as central to his way of thinking. I repeat a certain quote over and over in this book – "The action is in the reaction". I do this because this continuous action and reaction is the central thesis of the Alinsky model, and if you fail to understand this you will fail to understand Alinsky. If you fail to understand Alinsky, you will likely be defenseless against his tactics. Moreover, you will not be able to recognize them when they are used on the national stage.

# *Alinsky's Eleven Rules of the Ethics of Means and Ends*

Alinsky proposes eleven rules concerning the ethics of means and ends. I list them here with a short comment about each. I will then explain what I believe to be the problems and inconsistencies with Alinsky's argument, followed by a discussion of the morality of using the Alinsky tactics ourselves.

> I present here a series of rules pertaining to the ethics of means and ends: **first**, that one's concern with the ethics of means and ends varies inversely with one's personal interest in the issue. ...Accompanying this rule is the parallel one that one's concern with the ethics of means and ends varies inversely with one's distance from the scene of conflict.[11]

**In his first rule concerning the ethics of means and ends**, Alinsky is addressing the "not in my backyard" idea of situational ethics. For example, people vote for prisons, but then don't want a prison built near them. Likewise, Alinsky contends that people are much more likely to be concerned about issues that affect their lives and with issues that arise close to home.

Obviously, these statements are true, but does that mean that people will actually change their moral compass based solely on how near the issue is to them or how much it affects them or people they love directly? To Alinsky, perhaps this makes sense. I contend that while these factors might affect people to some extent, it is not likely to alter their core beliefs. Can anyone envision that the average person would actually result to murder because a political issue affects them directly? I'm cynical, but even I'm not that cynical.

**The second rule** of the ethics of means and ends is that the judgment of the ethics of means and ends is dependent upon the political position of those sitting in judgment.

He cites the use of extreme methods such as assassination by the Resistance in Hitler's Germany as examples of how people's sense of morality and ethics would be changed by the political circumstances in which they find themselves. He also mentions the Declaration of Independence and how it is essentially a declaration of war. He points out that the methods of the founding Fathers would seem extreme by today's standards. Of course, he is correct but he misses the point entirely. As with many of his rules of the ethics of means and ends, Alinsky equates the need for political change in America to much more dire circumstances in history. Hitler and the American Revolution are examples of boiling points in world history. It is absurd to think that one should use such extreme tactics in situations that clearly do not warrant it. With logic like this, Alinsky would find himself in the position of arguing that parents at little league games would be justified in assaulting the umpire if he makes a call against their children.

**The third rule** of the ethics of means and ends is that in war the end justifies almost any means.

Alinsky cites Winston Churchill's remarks to his secretary after she asked him if he would find it difficult to support

Russia during World War 2 after being such a strong anti-communist. He replied,

> "Not at all. I have only one purpose, the destruction of Hitler, and my life is much simplified thereby. If Hitler invaded Hell I would make at least a favorable reference to the Devil in the House of Commons."[12]

He also reminds us that President Lincoln had no problem suspending habeas corpus or using military trials on civilians if necessary. Again, all of this is true, but these things happened during war, not because a community organizer was upset about the conditions in some part of an American city.

**The fourth rule** of the ethics of means and ends is that judgment must be made in the context of the times in which the action occurred and not from any other chronological vantage point.

Here, Alinsky recalls Sam Adams and the Sons of Liberty, Abraham Lincoln's actions during the Civil War, and Thomas Jefferson's change in position regarding national self-interest after becoming President. His point is that different times call for different actions. This rule is essentially no different than his "everything is fair in love and war" argument, and my response is the same as above.

**The fifth rule** of ethics of means and ends is that concern with ethics increases with the number of means available and vice versa.

Alinsky recounts a time when he was embroiled in a conflict with a corporation, and people hired by the corporation caught Alinsky in a sexual indiscretion with a young woman. When they threatened to reveal his affair, Alinsky came forward and said,

> Go ahead and give it to the press. I think she's beautiful and I have never claimed to be celibate. Go ahead!
>
> Shortly afterwards, someone came forward from within the corporation to offer Alinsky information about a leader of the opposition who was caught in a homosexual indiscretion. Alinsky refused to use the information, "Thanks, but forget it. I don't fight that way. I don't want to see it. Goodbye." Alinsky confesses that he would have used the information if it had been the only means available to him.[13]

Alinsky does not base his objection to using such tactics on some sense of morality, but rather, on the perceived morality of the people he is trying to influence. This is an important point. Where most Conservatives would base their actions on their sense of some absolute moral standard, Alinsky teaches his followers to use the method that is perceived as most moral by the people most important to accomplishing the goal. The object is not to act a certain way because it is right. The object is to act a certain way because it will garner you the most support for your cause. In other words, expedience trumps morality, or perhaps more correctly – creates the morality. Alinsky's crusade against poverty is based on the moral imperative that one must act when confronted with those who are poor and lack political power. Where does Alinsky get this morality? Apparently, he gets it out of thin air, and then discards it when it becomes inconvenient to his "noble" cause.

**The sixth rule** of ethics of means and ends is that the less important the end to be desired, the more one can afford to engage in ethical evaluations of means.

Alinsky offers no comment on this rule, and it is no wonder because it is merely another way to state the same thing as previous rules. Like in times of war, not only is there an acceptance of broader means to affect the desired ends, but the time and effort to consider the means are reduced. No one who wants to make it through the war alive is going to stop on the battlefield to contemplate the moral implications of their actions.

**The seventh rule** of the ethics of means and ends is that generally success or failure is a mighty determinant of ethics.

This is basically the concept that history is written by the winners. Alinsky goes on to say, "There can be no such thing as a successful traitor, for if one succeeds he becomes a founding father."[14] This argument is not without merit. It is true that what future generations believe about a time in history will be greatly influenced by the fact that it is the victorious people that will tell the story of what happened. Of course, this was truer in the past than it is now. Today, information travels at the speed of light, and the record of what happens is saved via a myriad of devices such as video cameras, smart phones, computers, and more.

**The eighth rule** of the ethics of means and ends is that the morality of a means depends upon whether the means is being employed at a time of imminent defeat or imminent victory.

Alinsky's support of this rule is interesting because it demonstrates a tactic commonly used by Alinsky and by the community organizers who follow his teachings. He uses World War II as an example. Was it the right thing to do to use atomic weapons at the end of World War II? Of course, the justification that President Truman used for dropping the bombs on Japan was that it saved more lives than it took. Japan was not likely to surrender before being completely destroyed. The sheer enormity of the destruction from only two bombs caused Japan to blink.

Knowing that he was not likely to get much support for any argument that the United States had acted badly by dropping atomic bombs to prevent a protracted war, Alinsky instead uses a hypothetical to make his case. He proposes that if we had possessed the bomb at the time the Japanese attacked Pearl Harbor, we would have used that weapon against Japan to prevent a world war. This is a common tactic. If you can't make the case sufficiently by a proven example, then create a hypothetical that illustrates your point. It is another way to create a straw man. Alinsky never addresses the idea that desperation is a human reaction, and that anyone in possession of superior power is to be held to a higher ethical standard. Apparently, Alinsky is claiming not to see that there are levels of immoral behavior.

It is also interesting to note that this rule is a kind of moral declaration. He sees the gradation between times of imminent victory and times of imminent defeat, but he somehow cannot see that morality can come in shades. The inability to recognize that different circumstances may call for different actions, but that those actions are still subject to the ultimate test of absolute morality is baffling. One need not discard moral absolutes to understand that people act in gradations of moral turpitude.

**The ninth rule** of the ethics of means and ends is that any effective means is automatically judged by the opposition as being unethical.

Throughout the history of warfare, there have been rules to one extent or another. During the American Civil War, many Generals were referred to as having fought a 'Gentlemanly' campaign. It is just as true that different countries have been thought of as having engaged in barbaric practices in modern warfare. It sounds odd, perhaps, to classify people in such a way when the object is to kill your enemy, but there is an honor to war. The Geneva Conventions attempted to codify what is and what is not accepted in a time of war. The Geneva Conventions are defined as,

> The Geneva Conventions comprise four treaties, and three additional protocols, that establish the standards of international law for the humanitarian treatment of the victims of war. The singular term Geneva Convention denotes the agreements of 1949, negotiated in the aftermath of the Second World War (1939–45), which updated the terms of the first three treaties (1864, 1906, 1929), and added a fourth treaty. The articles of the Fourth Geneva Convention (1949) extensively defined the basic rights of prisoners (civil and military) during war; established protections for the wounded; and established protections for the civilians in and around a war zone. The treaties of 1949 were ratified, in whole or with reservations, by 194 countries.[15]

But what are the Geneva Conventions at heart? They are a written manifestation of the fact that even during such brutal times as war; mankind finds certain acts to be beyond the pale. Even in its basest moments, mankind takes time to ensure that only the level of suffering that must occur does occur. If we really lived by the maxim, "All's fair in love and war", we would have no Geneva Conventions, and no divorce courts for that matter. Man is constantly trying to reach his higher and nobler nature, not his lower and baser.

**The tenth rule** of the ethics of means and ends is that you do what you can with what you have and clothe it with moral garments.

There is no question that Alinsky has a valid point when he points out that people often try to clothe their otherwise inexcusable behavior in terms that make them look their best. He even quotes Lenin when he said,

> The task of the Bolsheviks is to overthrow the Imperialist Government. But this government rests upon the support of the Social Revolutionaries and Mensheviks, who in turn are supported by the trustfulness of the masses of people. We are in the minority. In the circumstances, there can be no talk of violence on our side...They have the guns and therefore we are for peace and for reformation through the ballot. When we have the guns then it will be through the bullet."[16]

The irony here, of course, is that it is the far-Left that has created oppressive nations such as the Soviet Union and not the far-Right. Undoubtedly, someone will chime in here with a Hitler reference, and I would remind them that Hitler came to power through the National Socialist Party. Jonah Goldberg has an excellent book entitled *Liberal Fascism*. I would recommend this book to the reader even if he or she were not confused regarding Hitler. It is an excellent telling of how socialism and communism have taken root and how the Progressive Party in this country is striving to dig it back up from the ash heap of history even today.

As I've noted, history is written by the victors, and it is human nature to put the best possible spin on things, but to claim that people always act without consideration for anyone else, brings cynicism to an entirely new level. It is said that Truman agonized with the idea of dropping the bombs on Hiroshima and Nagasaki, but determined that to not do so would prolong the war, cost hundreds of thousands of lives, and end up decimating the entire nation of Japan. Likewise, Lyndon Johnson was said to stay up night after night in fits of illness, calling the Pentagon repeatedly, to find out how many of "our sons" has been lost. Every President who has sent men into combat has agonized over his decision both before and after. I cannot imagine a single one of them callously choosing to undertake some war on a foreign soil merely in the hopes that he could clothe his decision in moral arguments at a later date. The cynicism with which Alinsky views the world is at once sad and frightening.

One wonders, were he alive today, if Alinsky would subject Obama's decisions to increase troop levels in Afghanistan, to bomb Libya or to take out Osama Bin Laden to the same level of skepticism, as that to which George W. Bush was subjected in the preceding eight years. Would Alinsky, were he alive today, be castigating Obama, and claiming that he is acting out of some Super

Power unilateralism just to clothe his decisions in moral arguments after the fact? I somehow doubt it. And. so it is with the Left, Bush was an evil warmonger even though he got Congressional approval for his actions, but Obama is blameless when he did not.

Alinsky's tenth rule is not without some merit, and should be considered, but is mostly the thought of a victim. A victim who buys into the conspiracy theories surrounding Government in an attempt to explain away difficult decisions, horrific acts, and circumstances that do not fit within their own personal paradigms. To suggest that every moment of progress that has ever occurred to the betterment of man is simply the result of someone deciding that they could get away with it, and then claim that it was the right thing to do, is ludicrous. Did Martin Luther King Jr. begin his crusade for justice for blacks in America with the idea that he would just do as he pleases, and hope to clothe it in moral garb later? Did Jesus only set out to die on the cross in hopes that he could morally assuage people of his correctness later? I guess Alinsky could have envisioned Gandhi with a machine gun, or Mother Theresa with an RPG. Some of Alinsky's teachings just leave us scratching our heads. If Alinsky had lived, he probably would have been trying to arm Occupy Wall Street with weapons, and encouraging people to bring munitions to Palestine.

**The eleventh rule** of the ethics of means and ends is that goals must be phrased in general terms like "Liberty, Equality, Fraternity, and" "Of the Common Welfare,""Pursuit of Happiness, "or "Bread and Peace."

Before we begin our discussion here, were you able to read that last rule without thinking of Barack Obama. I mean, after all, what was "hope and change", and "change you can believe in" if not phrasing goals in general terms?

It is interesting to note that Alinsky's discussion of the final rule is all about the fact that one means might lead to another valuable or desirable end. For example, Alinsky says,

> It has been previously noted that the wise man of action, knows that frequently in the stream of action of means towards ends, whole new and unexpected ends are among the major results of the action. From a Civil War fought as a means to preserve the Union came the end of slavery.[17]

His point is that the community organizer might not immediately see all of the good that can come from his action, and so he should couch his terms in generalities to allow for other, unforeseen ends. Of course, this is exactly what Obama did in the 2008 Presidential campaign. By being purposefully vague, he could claim to be unaccountable if he fails to deliver. Moreover, he can anticipate that there may be things that come about later that will be desirable, and he can claim these were the very things he meant by "hope and change".

Unfortunately, "hope and change" is not a plan. You can't get "hope and change" through Congress. So, Obama is stuck with a generality into which he has to pour bad news, not good. As I will mention again later, Alinsky tactics are pretty effective for a candidate running for office, but they fall woefully short for a President seeking to govern.

# The Fallacy of Alinsky's Moral Argument

Even common sense, if not our religious conviction, can lead us to understand that while ends are desirable, not all means are morally acceptable. Alinsky makes a great deal of the fact that if man is put into the most horrific circumstance possible, that he will likely use any means at his disposal without consideration of its morality. This is probably true. A man starved long enough, will likely eat his shoe, but a man who merely has to skip lunch is not likely to do so. There are degrees of desperation. Not every situation calls for the direst of solutions. Can Alinsky really argue that because such extreme behavior can take place, that his own preconceived notion of the necessity of a Marxist revolution demands that such behavior should take place? I think not, and I think most reasonable thinking people will agree with me. While we are aghast that the Donner Party chose to eat their dead, on some level we understand that they did what they did to survive. It is far from morally equivalent to eat your roommate because you don't have enough money for groceries. While we admire those with the gumption to go into a hostile area, stake a claim, and work it for the gold it grudging gives forth, I doubt that many of us would suggest that the intrinsic value of gold makes it equally acceptable to put a bullet in your friend's head for his share. Alinsky argues for intrinsic values, but isn't everything only of value insomuch as it can provide something useful to us? Even gold is no good if you're hungry and there is no food to purchase. I'm certain you would gladly trade some gold for food if you were starving. So nothing is intrinsically valuable, it derives its value from its ability to be used or transferred for something useful.

So, when Alinsky talks of revolution, he speaks of it in terms of life and death. He acts as though the absence of his particular brand of revolution makes life itself completely void of meaning. This is interesting in light of his propensity for late night drinking, fancy restaurants, keeping company with famous crime figures, spending time with women of all kinds, and his ever-increasing, all-consuming need to be known and respected.[18] Wouldn't his time be spent more efficaciously in the pursuit of his stated goals? Wouldn't it make more sense that he would have only the very least money possible to be an example to the downtrodden he sought to reach? Why would he be so concerned (as he was) that his books did not sell as well as he thought they should? While decrying inequity, he enjoyed the good life, rubbing shoulders with the rich and the makers and shakers of the world. While he preached of revolution, he immersed himself, not in the world as it should be, but in the world as it is. This does not seem like a man who is driven to revolution out of necessity.

We have to decide if every injustice rises to a level requiring that the most extreme means be employed. It's as though Alinsky is saying wrong is wrong, and so any means necessary to right that wrong is acceptable. Leaving aside for the moment that Alinsky provides absolutely no standard by which we should consider something to be wrong, can we really claim that every infraction is equal? Would any sane person say that a five-year-old stealing a candy bar is the same as flying commercial airliners into the World Trade Centers or the Pentagon? I should think not. Would anyone really suggest that the same punishment be meted out? Are we to begin sending children who steal candy to Gitmo? Should we put to death a teenager who steals a car for a joyride? Should jaywalkers get life in prison? Yet this is the type of moral equivalency that Alinsky would have us accept. On top of this ridiculousness, Alinsky seems driven by a moral imperative that society is wrong, and yet unable to accept that there is such a thing as "wrong". He is trapped in a moral paradox, and his arguments do nothing to extricate him.

Alinsky fails to see varying levels of "wrongness". Alinsky is so fired up about his revolution that to him, there is nothing more important. In speaking of the revolution, Alinsky quotes Christ in saying, "He that is not with me, is against me". He takes his ambition to help those in poverty not only to the national level, but to the level of God and morality. To him, to fail to act when others are in need is as great a sin as anything of which he can think, and so failing to join him in revolution is akin to committing the most heinous of crimes. This inability to see gradations in wrong-doing forces Alinsky to twist and contort the little speckles of legitimate philosophical thoughts he sprinkles throughout his treatise. This type of lazy, pseudo-intellectual nonsense may have played well to the teenagers and college kids to whom he spoke, but it falls short when subjected to thoughtful analysis.

There are levels of wrong. It is not the same to jaywalk as it is to kill your spouse. It is not the same to fail to pay a parking ticket as it is to commit a rape. It is not the same to have a library book out too long as it is to assassinate a President. When he acts as though the so-called evils of capitalism rise to the level that they demand justice by any means necessary, he insults our intelligence, and assaults our senses. We cannot simply say that someone has done something wrong, and therefore we should use any means at our disposal to stop them. An intelligent person must first be convinced that the level of the infraction lives up to the proposed level of justice to be meted out. On this count, Alinsky fails miserably.

Alinsky is left with his moral paradox. On one hand, he is compelled by the immorality of the inequitable distribution of wealth, and yet he finds no moral hazard at all in attempting to change this inequity by means of lies, ridicule, misrepresentation, or any other unethical means at his disposal. To Alinsky, the need to win the war outweighs the need to abide by moral means, and yet it is morality that creates the need to act in the first place. Where does Alinsky derive this morality that compels him to change the world? If there is such a morality, would it not also compel him to use moral means? If there is no morality, then what is the motivation for his revolution?

Instead, Alinsky relies on his own unique brand of moral relativism, but even this fails to create a coherent philosophy of ethics. Where do we draw the line with such moral relativism? For example, if you felt that a President did not support your point of view, would you be justified in having him or her assassinated? Of course not! However, if you follow Alinsky, you would be hard pressed to explain why assassination would be wrong. By claiming this dualism of his, that is the existence of both God and Satan in all of us, Alinsky gives himself a 'get out of jail free card'. Whenever the philosophy doesn't fit him, he simply declares himself to be a dualistic human being. Unfortunately, in the real world, you get arrested for doing things wrong, and your favorite philosopher of the moment is not going to set you free.

## *Should We use Alinsky Tactics or Not?*

The bottom line with Alinsky tactics comes down to common sense and a common sense of decency. While many Conservatives will turn to the Bible for their sense of morality, and this is fine, it need not be that complicated. After all, we all know it's wrong to lie, and to treat others unfairly. When Alinsky tactics cross a line of common decency, then they are to be eschewed. It doesn't take a dispensation from on high to make us aware that treating other people unfairly is wrong. Revealing the tactics for what they are causes no moral dilemma at all. However, using the tactics can call our sense of morality into play. In the end, everyone must decide for themselves how far they are willing to go to defeat Alinsky tactics. We know that the other side will not be assuaged by the need to behave morally. Defeating evil often comes at a steep price, and it is worth noting that when we fight for what we believe to be right without consideration for the means we use in that fight, we become no better than those we seek to defeat.

There are certain things that I believe we can all agree are morally reprehensible. If we lie or knowingly spread false information about others, it seems obvious that such actions are wrong. Inciting people to violence or fabricating information, likewise, seem clearly wrong. Any hint of racism or sexism is clearly wrong. However, there are certain aspects of Alinsky's tactics that are not so clear. Is it acceptable to ridicule someone? There is no question that using Alinsky tactics can cause us to walk a moral tightrope, but many of the tactics can be employed without offending the conscience. Additionally, I offer an entire chapter on principles that can be used to defeat Alinsky tactics without violating our sense of morality.

If you are willfully misrepresenting someone, then it's wrong. If you are simply finding creative ways to expose someone's wrong doing then it certainly is not. The moral parameters within which each of us is willing to operate will vary slightly, but we should not stoop to their level. We should never simply call names, incite violence, or otherwise engage in any of a host of other things that the Left finds no problem with. Let common sense, and common decency be your guide. To the Alinskyite, it is victory at any cost and by any means necessary. To the rest of us, victory is our goal, but the way we achieve that victory is important as well. They may believe the ends justify the means, but we must be better than that. We must work harder, and find ways to beat them at their own game without losing our souls in the process.

As far as the end justifying the means – there is a common thread in this ideology. It is present in all the political philosophies that have arisen to offer an antithetical choice to American Democracy. I would encourage the reader to study the use of "ends justify the means" philosophy in Leninism and Radical Islam. In the meantime, we should understand Alinsky tactics, and use them with caution. While using some of the tactics will not be morally problematic, others create difficulties. It is good to understand the tactics, know how to defend against them, and in some cases use them yourself. Rather than using many of the tactics, it would probably be better simply to learn them and then apply the principles I set forth in chapter four.

# 3

# THE 13 MAIN ALINSKY TACTICS EXPLAINED

*"If you know the enemy and know yourself, you need not fear the result of a hundred battles. If you know yourself but not the enemy, for every victory gained you will also suffer a defeat. If you know neither the enemy nor yourself, you will succumb in every battle"* — Sun Tzu, The Art of War

## *Understanding the Intent*

In *Rules for Radicals*, Alinsky has a chapter entitled "Tactics". This chapter does not include all Alinsky tactics. In fact, we will see more in the final chapter, but the 13 listed in this chapter form the core of the Alinsky model, and it is these 13 tactics or rules I will attempt to explain in this chapter. I offer no advice here on how to combat them, and I engage in very little discussion here of the moral ramifications of Alinsky's methods. I will deal with defeating the tactics in the following chapter, and I have already dealt with the moral ramifications of the tactics in the previous chapter. Here we simply seek to understand what the tactics are, and the ability to recognize them when they are used. If you study this chapter carefully, your eyes will be opened to the forces driving the actions of President Obama and his advisers. It is sad but true that understanding Alinsky makes sense of the Obama Administration, and even allows you, to some extent, to predict what they will do next. Without *Rules for Radicals*, the Obama Administration's actions might seem haphazard, disjointed, and counterintuitive. However, when you view their actions through the prism of Alinsky principles your eyes are opened, you begin to understand the rationale behind what they are doing, and you can begin to see what they will be doing.

Remember that the Alinsky model is intended to tear down, not to build up. His stated purpose was,

> WHAT FOLLOWS IS for those who want to change the world from what it is to what they believe it should be. The Prince was written by Machiavelli for the Haves on how to hold power. *Rules for Radicals* is written for the Have-Nots on how to take it away.[19]

## *Thirteen Tactics Woven Together*

To understand the Alinsky tactics it is critical to understand that they are not intended as a cookbook of tactics to be applied to every specific circumstance, but as a general reference manual for organizers. Alinsky never intended that organizers should attempt to apply the rules, hard and fast, to every circumstance they encountered. One of the key elements of Alinsky's methodology was adaptability. Alinsky wrote of community organizers he had trained,

> Among the organizers I trained and failed with, there were some who memorized the words and the related experiences and concepts. Listening to them was like listening to a tape playing back my presentation word for word. Clearly, there was little understanding; clearly, they could not do more than elementary organization. The problem with so many of them was and is their failure to understand that a statement of a specific situation is significant only in its relationship to and its illumination of a general concept. Instead, they see the specific action as a terminal point. They find it difficult to grasp the fact that no situation ever repeats itself, that no tactic can be precisely the same.[20]

And again,

> I hesitate to spell out specific application of these tactics. I remember an unfortunate experience with my Reveille for Radicals [Alinsky's first book on community organizing], in which I collected accounts of particular actions and tactics employed in organizing a number of communities. For some time after the book was published I got reports that would-be organizers were using this book as a manual, and whenever they were confronted with a puzzling situation they would retreat into some vestibule or alley and thumb through to find the answer! There can be no prescriptions for particular situations because the same situation rarely

recurs, and more than history repeats itself. People, pressures, and patterns of power are variables, and a particular combination exists only in a particular time – even then, the variables are constantly in a state of flux. *Tactics must be understood as specific applications of the rules and principles that I have listed above*. It is the principles that the organizer must carry with him in battle. To these he applies his imagination, and he relates them tactically to specific situations.[21]

The 13 rules outlined in this chapter, and taken directly from the chapter in *Rules for Radicals* entitled, "Tactics", are the bones of the Alinsky model. The flesh must be created in response to the specific circumstances faced by the individual organizer. The exact same can be said for my approach to the principles to defeat Alinsky tactics outlined in the following chapter. My explanations below are intended to give you a flavor of the tactics, and how they may be used, and/or have been used. This is not intended as a reference manual for every situation. To Alinsky, the only successful organizers were those who could think on their feet, and think creatively enough to take the tactics he outlined and find new and ingenious ways to apply them to ever changing conditions. You must understand the tactics in order to defeat them, but understanding them alone is not sufficient for victory. The shop worn phrase, "thinking outside the box" applies here. Rote memorization of Alinsky tactics will never provide the solutions to defeat the Alinsky model anymore than it would provide sufficient solutions for successful community organizing. Learning to use the Alinsky model and learning to defeat the Alinsky model is as much an art as it is a science. In later chapters, we will examine creative methods for defeating the tactics. Even these methods, however, will never be sufficient to serve as a "cookbook" for battling Alinsky tactics. As circumstances change, the ways in which people employ the tactics will change. This, in turn, will require that you be adaptable and resilient enough to find creative ways to use the principles I will outline to defeat the Alinsky tactics.

There are some overarching principles implicit in the tactics that act as the glue that bind the tactics into one cohesive unit. The following three quotes from Alinsky will help to illustrate these overarching principles:

> The real action is in the enemy's reaction.
>
> The enemy properly goaded and guided in his reaction will be your major strength.
>
> Tactics, like organization, like life, require that you move with the action.[22]

In our approach to understanding, Alinsky's methods as he used them, and as they have been refined for use in the current political environment, we can encapsulate in one sentence the web that holds the entire model together. Memorize it!

**The driving force of the Alinsky model is in the action, specifically in guiding the action in such a way that you cause your "enemy" to react rather than act.**

I highly recommend that you stop, reread, and consider the implications of the previous sentence, because it is the single most important prerequisite for understanding both how to use, as well as how to defeat the Alinsky model.

The intent of the tactics is to keep your enemy off balance. Whether by mockery, subterfuge, or any other available strategy, the purpose behind the tactics is to keep the pressure on your opponent, constantly jabbing and goading them until they lose their clarity of thought, and react in a way that you can exploit to defeat them. Again from *Rules for Radicals*,

> The job then is getting the people to move, to act, to participate; in short, to develop and harness the necessary power to effectively conflict with the prevailing patterns and change them. When those prominent in the status quo turn and label you an "agitator", they are completely correct, for that is, in one word, your function – to agitate to the point of conflict.[23]

In an interview with Studs Terkel, Alinsky defined himself as a "professional outside agitator". He went on to explain that you must be an outside agitator because one of two things happens to those who try to agitate from within – "either they get knocked off or they get co-opted".[24] And again from Rules for Radicals,

> *The first step in community organization is community disorganization.* The disruption of the present organization is the first step toward community organization. Present arrangements must be disorganized if they are to be displaced by new patterns that provide the opportunities and means for citizen participation. All change means disorganization of the old and organization of the new.[25]

So, as we attempt to understand each of the 13 tactics outlined by Alinsky, let us be aware that the real driving force behind it all is, in one word – pressure. It is no wonder that those who use Alinsky methods, whether consciously or not, are inclined to do things like calling you a racist with absolutely no basis for doing so, or to insult you or deride you as unintelligent, inarticulate or uninformed. Whatever particular approach they choose, the intent is to goad you into reacting. If you remember nothing else from this book, remember this,

## The action is in the reaction.

One last thought before we begin to examine each of the rules one by one. As I explained previously, Alinsky did not self-identify, specifically so he could be that "outside" agitator he spoke of in his interview with Studs Terkel. As such, it is pointless to call him a Marxist, because any Liberal familiar in the least with Alinsky will immediately remind you that Alinsky never claimed to be a Marxist. However, if you are familiar with Marxism and the terminology often employed by Marx, Engels, and others you will be struck by how Alinsky comes back repeatedly to the familiar Marxist vocabulary. Obviously, a serious discussion of Marxism is beyond the scope of this book, but I would encourage you to familiarize yourself with it. Read Das Kapital and the Communist Manifesto, and then come back to Alinsky, and see if you don't recognize the nomenclature. In fact, read Marxist literature, and revisit the speeches of Barack Obama, and see if you can't recognize why he would say in his own book that he "sought out…Marxist professors".

As an aside, if you are discussing any connections President Obama might have to Marxism on twitter or Facebook, there is one sure way to recognize that you are conversing with a member of Organizing for America (OFA). If you mention Marx, and they make some allegedly humorous remark that the only Marx they are familiar with is Groucho, you can bet you're dealing with OFA. This is one of their canned responses. I will revisit the OFA and other social media subjects in an upcoming booklet.

## *A Practical Guide*

In the discussion that follows, my intent is to familiarize you with each of the tactics, and to provide you with some concrete examples of how each of them has been used. This is not intended to be an exhaustive study of the rules and all their implications. It is intended as a practical guide to help you recognize the tactics when you see them being used. As we discussed above, there can be no comprehensive guide to the tactics, or to defeating them. They are designed to be amorphous enough to be tweaked creatively to apply to as many different situations as possible. The way the tactics are used will depend upon the variables of the situation, the skill of the person using the tactics, and the medium in which the tactics are being employed. Likewise, your ability to counteract and defeat the use of Alinsky tactics will depend upon your understanding of the tactics, your understanding of the overarching principles of the Alinsky model, your understanding of the principles in the next chapter, your creativity, and the medium in which you are interacting.

The rest of this chapter will provide you with a basic understanding of the Alinsky tactics. If you just want to be able to recognize them when they are being used, this chapter should be sufficient to that end. If you want to be truly effective at defeating Alinsky tactics, it will require a careful reading of this chapter and the following chapter. To truly be adept at defeating the Alinsky model you must be willing to study hard, and practice often (twitter is an excellent place to practice). Don't skip this chapter. Understand it fully before you attempt to counteract the methods as they are used against you. Without a firm grasp of what each of the rules means, you will be unable to recognize the tactic(s) you are dealing with, and it takes a thorough understanding of the intent of the rules to build successful strategies for defeating them. Seek to know the rules so well that you instantly recognize them. It may take a couple of readings of these explanations before you truly understand them well enough to recognize them in use. Once you understand them thoroughly, you are then ready to move on to the chapters that deal with counteracting them.

# *The 13 Tactics Explained*

## Rule 1 - Power is not only what you have but what the enemy thinks you have.

### *Explanation*

In the chapter of *Rules for Radicals* entitled *Tactics*, Alinsky states his first rule as,

> "Power is not only what you have but what the enemy thinks you have".

The quote at the head of the chapter on tactics is, *"We will either find a way or make one." - Hannibal*[26]

As I mentioned in the previous chapter, moral dualism is his way of allowing the devil on one shoulder to hold as much sway over his thoughts and actions as does the angel on the other shoulder. However, what we see in Alinsky, and what we see typified in the first rule, is not dualism as much as duplicity, and Alinsky alerts us to his willingness to embrace his duplicity with the very first rule. After all, what is Alinsky really saying? He is saying that it doesn't matter who you are, it only matters who people think you are. In Alinsky's mind, to hide behind a mask is completely acceptable so long as you have the proper end in mind. Of course, as we saw in the previous chapter, the end may justify the means for Alinsky, but he fails to take into account that he is choosing the ends for his followers. He becomes de facto king, dictator, and chief of the thought police simply by claiming that what he seeks to accomplish is the right thing, and that even if it could be achieved another way it doesn't matter because so long as his ends are reached, nothing else matters.

The essence of Alinsky's first rule is that if you do not have the numbers or any real power, you can organize in such a way that you appear to have more power than you do. Marches and planned occupations like Occupy Wall Street are prime examples of this type of behavior. Occupy Wall Street claims to be the 99%, but in numbers, they are more like the .01%. With a complicit median, they are able to appear larger, and more influential than they truly are. Alinsky's point with the first rule is even if you don't have the numbers or the power, you can make it look like you do.

Power is not only what you have, but what the enemy thinks you have – while this may be effective, it is also dishonest. This is not "fake it until you make it", which is a valuable tool to correct your behavior. This is "fake it until you make them do it your way". He has no problem hiding behind a façade to reach his goals. He sees nothing morally corrupt about pretending to be what he is not in order to convince others to think and act in ways he deems appropriate.

By using a quote from Hannibal to start the chapter on tactics, Alinsky indicates his resolute nature once again. Hannibal is renowned as one of the greatest military minds in history, and his leadership of the Carthaginian military is the stuff of legends. His exploits included his march towards Rome, taking a Carthaginian army across the Pyrenees and the Alps – one of the most daring military strategies ever attempted against nearly overwhelming odds.[27] If anything characterized Alinsky and his mindset towards revolution, it was determination. Always keep in mind that the central tenet of the Alinsky tactics is summed up in his exposition of the tenth rule,

> "It is this unceasing pressure that results in the reactions from the opposition that are essential for the success of the campaign. **It should be remembered not only that the action is in the reaction but that action is itself the consequence of reaction and of reaction to reaction."**[28] [Emphasis added]

Again, "The action is in the reaction". Pressure, constant and adaptable, is the single biggest key to the Alinsky model, and it is the single biggest key to defeating that model as well.

Alinsky goes on to compare the use of tactics to the human face,

> "The eyes represent visible power such as is possessed by the ruling class. The ears represent a smaller group who cloaks their lack of size by raising a din that belies their numbers. Finally, he mentions the nose, "[I]f your organization is too tiny even for noise, stink up the place."[29]

The ears are what Alinsky is primarily speaking of in the first rule; lacking in size, they raise "a din that belies their numbers." In other words, you can make up for an insufficiency in numbers by being louder. We see this often when a small group raises a very loud protest, and thereby has undue influence. For example, a product or television program may offend a particular group, and even though the number of people who speak up is less than 1% of the target audience, their loud voice creates reactions beyond the power of their numbers.

His reference to "stinking up the place" has a real-life example. Alinsky recounts a tactic that he had suggested as a creative alternative to the same stale tactics he had seen activists using. His suggestion was to buy a hundred seats to a symphony concert in which the music was relatively quiet, and then select "a hundred blacks", feed them a dinner of baked beans and wait for the obvious consequences. He even quips, "The concert would be over before the first movement!"[30]

The point Alinsky is making is that with creativity and a willingness to be bold and brash, you can offset the lack of numbers or money. The revolution need not be hampered by its lack of actual power. Often, the illusion of power is just as effective, if not more so. Even the threat of a boycott can sometimes be so effective that a company is willing to make compromises rather than engage.

The first Alinsky tactic almost seems borrowed from nature where animals routinely do everything in their power to make themselves appear larger than they actually are in order to intimidate their enemies. Have you ever noticed a frightened cat? Its answer to a threat is to arch its back and stand its fur on end to appear as large as possible. In the absence of real power, a convincing act can often suffice quite well. The battle is in the reaction. If the enemy reacts to your carefully orchestrated attempt to convey the presence of power – well, the action is in the reaction, and you have created the reaction instead of being the one who is acted upon.

So then, the first rule is the art of managing perceptions. Alinsky assumes that he is speaking not to the ruling class, but to the smaller, disenfranchised groups that are seeking power. After all, Alinsky would posit, why would the ruling class want things to change at all? It is this "status quo" that the community organizer is challenged to turn on its head. Therefore, since the numbers of the oppressed are small, it is critical to find ways to seem larger than you are. Just because you aren't powerful doesn't mean that you can't convince others that you are. If you don't have the numbers, you can always make the most noise.

# Examples

Now, let us look at some examples of the way the first rule has been used.

### Obama's Symbolic Announcement to Run for President

In 2007, then Senator Barack Obama used Alinsky's first rule in his official announcement that he would seek the office President of the United States. As a little known Senator with an undistinguished record, Obama had no real record or power to display. Therefore, instead he used Alinsky's first rule and managed the people's perceptions in order to appear powerful. Taking Alinsky's analogy of the ears, Obama sought to make enough noise that his fledgling campaign would appear larger and more powerful than it was. Here's how he did it. First, he used symbolism. He stood before the Old State Capitol building in February of 2007 and declared himself a candidate for

President of the United States. An online newspaper described it in these words,

> "The first-term senator announced his candidacy from the state capital where he began his elective career just 10 years ago, and in front of the building where in another century, Lincoln served eight years in the Illinois Legislature."[31]

With a few thousand followers listening, the young Senator seized upon everything he could to make his movement seem bigger than it was. He mentioned Lincoln several times in his speech. This was effective because Lincoln is commonly thought to be the greatest President in American history. However, the power of the symbolism went well beyond that. As an African-American, standing in the very place where the man who had signed the Emancipation Proclamation into law began his career, Obama seemed to speak to the enormous possibilities that exist only because of the boldness of belief and the American spirit. His shrewd use of the 16th President, made Obama look like the inevitable culmination of all that Lincoln sought to accomplish. Never mind that Obama did not possess the slightest qualifications to be President, he appeared to, and power is not only what you have, but what the enemy thinks you have.

He also spoke about the war in Iraq, and bringing home our troops, in an effort to magnify his message. This speech took place in the first few weeks of the surge and in the midst of rising discontent over the war and over Bush's management of Iraq. He seized upon the issue that was garnering the highest percentage of mainstream media coverage, and married himself to it. Since Mr. Obama was not in the U.S. Senate when the resolution to give war powers to President Bush took place, he found himself in the unique position of speaking out against the war in Iraq without seeming hypocritical for having voted for the resolution. He would later exploit this as club to hammer Hillary Clinton, his more experienced opponent, who had been in the Senate at the time, and voted for the resolution.

### *The Fake Presidential Seal*

How many remember the fake Presidential seal from Obama's meeting in Chicago in June of 2008? It caused quite a stir as people felt that Obama was using a seal that looked far too much like the official Presidential seal. This is another example of perceived power. Candidates have always sought to "look Presidential" but many believe this crossed a line. In fact, some have opined that the seal used in this manner was in fact a violation of the law. The *Weekly Standard* explains that it is illegal to use the Presidential Seal when you are not in fact the President of the United States. (McCormack 2008)

If Obama's team did cross a line, they did so because they were following Alinsky rules, which do not consider anything, no matter how immoral, to be dirty tricks. Instead, moves like this are demonstrations of how committed someone is to their cause. The ends justify the means methodology of Alinsky can often lead to questionable acts like this. (Broder 2008)

### *The Office of the President Elect*

In an unprecedented move, Obama chose to set up what he called "The Office of the President Elect". Of course, there is in fact no such thing as an office of the President Elect, and it was merely an affectation to bestow perceived power on him before he actually had any real power. Few would argue that it was effective, and that no President Elect has ever had more effect on policy while not actually holding the office.

### *Obama vs. Hillary in the Caucus States*

Another example of Obama's use of the first rule is his method for attaining caucus victories. The Obama supporters were routinely louder and more aggressive than the delegates for the opposition were. It didn't matter if he had more delegates at the beginning of the process, as long as he had the loudest delegates they would eventually drown out the others and claim the victory, and this is exactly what they did.[32]

According to TalkLeft.com, they obtained a memo that illustrated the main tactics the Obama people used to overwhelm the opposition at caucuses. Here are the main points they brought out:

> Individuals arriving all at once in large groups can disrupt the caucus by making it difficult to keep track of sign-in sheets, among other things.
>
> Individuals may arrive who are not registered to vote in a particular precinct with the story that 'they just moved there.

> Supporters for a particular candidate, such as Senator Clinton, have arrived at caucus sites early to decorate and organize and been told that 'the building was locked.[33]

These are clear examples of power being not only what you have, but also what others perceive that you have. Obama used groups of loud, rowdy delegates (and possibly non-delegates) to make it seem as though his support was larger than it really was. Strong organization and avid supporters are often what lead to a caucus victory, but Obama's supporters were beyond the pale. Moreover, by stooping to dirty political tricks like locking the building, it not only kept the opposition out it also made Obama's people appear more powerful than Clinton's.

Since Clinton won in the bigger states such as Texas, Pennsylvania, and Florida (although Florida did not count at the time), it was critical for Obama to take the caucuses, and take them he did. Most believe that the caucuses swung the primary in favor of Obama, and without these tactics, Hillary Clinton would have been the Democratic nominee.[34]

# Summary

In describing what he means by tactics Alinsky says,

> "In the world of give and take, tactics is the art of how to take and how to give. Here our concern is with the tactic of taking; how the Have-Nots can take power away from the Haves."[35]

The Alinsky model is designed to provide power to those who don't already possess it. It is the Marxist idea of the proletariat rising up and casting off the oppressive bourgeoisie. Since Alinsky's emphasis is on helping the lower class, he realizes that some special tactics will have to be employed. After all, the lower classes possess neither the prestige nor the money to affect any real change. They must rely on other methods. The first of these methods is to manage the art of perception, and to use sheer numbers when possible to offset the entrenched power and wealth of the upper class. If the lower class sees itself as powerless to create change, they will not be mobilized to overthrow the rich so Alinsky redefines power to be not only what you have, but also what others think you have. The art of the bluff and the ability to manage perceptions, to favor those whom Alinsky saw as disenfranchised from the American dream, form the first general principle for the successful agitator.

## Rule 2 - Never Go Outside the Experience of Your People

## Explanation

Alinsky states the second rule as,

> The second rule is - Never go outside the experience of your people.

> When an action or tactic is outside the experience of the people, the result is confusion, fear, and retreat. It also means a collapse of communication, as we have noted.[36]

This rule, like most of the Alinsky tactics, is really just a common sense idea that had never been applied in quite this way. Putting this rule more succinctly – play to your strengths. Genius in its simplicity, the second tactic reminds us that it's always better to play to your own strengths rather than allow your opponent to draw you into their area of strength. Think of it like a football team – when you play to your strengths it's like having the home field advantage. When you don't - it's like playing on the road all the time. A team with a strong running game should stick with its strength even if it is unsuccessful early in the game. Likewise, a team whose strength is in their defense should not be taking many risks offensively. In football, as in life, you are much more likely to be successful playing to your own strengths. The point of tactics two and three is to remind "radicals" that they will always be more effective when they play to their strengths.

Likewise, as a leader, the community organizer should not be placing people in the wrong position. Again, as in football, it would be like telling your defensive line to play offensive line and your running back to play quarterback. They would be out of their comfort zones, and much less effective.

Consider then the consequences Alinsky spells out for failing to uphold the second rule. First, when venturing outside of your area of experience, you are likely to become confused. This seems only natural. After all, people tend to operate in comfort zones developed by years of experience at doing similar or identical things. One man may be a master craftsman when it comes to carpentry, but take that same talented man and instead tell him he must now be a glass blower, and you are certain to confuse him. We all operate better under circumstances with which we are familiar, and tend to become confused when confronted with the unknown. Likewise, in political battles it is always best to use your people where they have proven that they are strong. Don't allow the other side to lure you into battling them in areas where you are not strong. Why do you think politicians always attempt to turn questions back to their own talking points? The questioner wants to expose the weakness of the politician, and the politician is determined to redirect everything he or she is asked back to their talking points.

Second, operating outside of your normal comfort zone can lead to fear. For example, let's suppose you were at a Tea Party rally. Everyone around you has generally the same philosophy and concerns that you do. Now suppose instead that you are at a meeting of the New Black Panthers and you are the only Conservative in attendance (which you are likely to be). How would you behave differently in these two very different situations? It seems obvious that you would feel not only comfortable, but also bold with those with whom you agree. On the other hand, you would likely feel confused, be a bit fearful and would be anxious to get out of the Black Panther meeting.

Third, alienation from the familiar leads to retreat. The point Alinsky is making is that when you are not operating in the realm of your greatest experience you become less confident, and find yourself much more likely to beat a hasty retreat. When you're talking about a subject over which you have mastery, you are confident and bold. You are unafraid to express your ideas and opinions. However, when you are forced to discuss a subject about which you know little, your first thought is to disengage. People who are confident in what they are doing maintain a constant offensive against their opponents, while people forced to act in situation with which they are not comfortable are likely to retreat and play defense. Using the right people for the right tasks is critical to success.

Fourth, and perhaps least intuitively, operating outside of your area of experience can lead to a lack of communication. Alinsky illustrates the point in *Rules for Radicals* in the chapter entitled *"Communication"*. He tells the story of how he had to illustrate this concept to some radicals he was training.

They were eating breakfast at a restaurant when Alinsky pointed out that everything on the menu had a corresponding number associated with it. He confidently pronounced that he would demonstrate that the waiter was so accustomed to operating under the assumption that he could write out an order with only a number and perhaps a slight modification that he would be unable to adapt if forced to act outside of his usual comfort zone. For example, if number one was eggs and bacon, he could simply say, "Number one, over easy". Alinsky then went on to prove his point. Number 6 was a chicken liver omelet, but when he ordered it, and the waiter had responded with a, "Yes, No. 6", Alinsky then said, "Well, just a minute. I don't want the chicken livers in the omelet. I want the omelet with the chicken livers on the side – now, is that clear?"

Alinsky goes on, "He will say it is, and then the odds are 9 to 1 everything is going to get screwed up because he can't just order No. 6 anymore. I don't know what will happen, but I have gone outside his accepted area of experience."

The result was that Alinsky wound up with a full order of chicken livers and an omelet, and a bill for both. After he complained to the manager, he received an apology and a discount. Alinsky recalls, "Waiter and manager huddled. Finally, the waiter returned, flushed and upset: "Sorry about the mistake – everybody got mixed up – eat whatever you want." The bill was charged back to the original price for No. 6."[37]

# Examples

If you want to be successful, operate as often as possible in your comfort zone, and use your people only in areas where they feel comfortable. This is exactly what Barack Obama and his advisors did in the 2008 campaign.

There were times when it seemed like Bill Ayers, Tony Rezko, or Jeremiah Wright would be the associations that brought the Obama campaign down, but the stubbornly refused to allow anyone to draw them into protracted discussions in their areas of weakness. If you asked about Bill Ayers, it was "guilt by association", and after all, he was just "some guy from his neighborhood".

Only once did anything come close to pulling Obama off message and into a battle in area of his weakness – the Jeremiah Wright controversy. When it became public knowledge that Obama had sat in the pews of a church for 20 years where a pastor had proclaimed, "God damn America", the Obama team was in trouble. This is the only time during the entire campaign where Obama was forced to go off message, and address questions about him.

You will recall that the answer was to essentially throw Wright under the bus, play down his association with him, and instead use the opportunity for a speech on racial tolerance. Surrounded by more American flags than most would have believed could fit on a television screen, Obama proceeded to use the Jeremiah Wright story as an opportunity to discuss racial relations. Even though he never answered the question of how he could sit in that church for so many years, and not know what the Pastor believed, he came away from that speech with the Liberal media echoing in a chorus that Barack Obama had done more to heal America's racial divide than anyone since Martin Luther King Jr.

Skillful use of Alinsky tactics allowed the Obama campaign team to extricate themselves from what could have been a campaign killer. Instead, they played to their strengths, and it worked.

Finally, the key thing to watch for to spot this rule in action is the avoidance of the subject at hand. When Alinskyites are trapped due to their flawed logic and/or policies, they flee to the safety of the red herring. If you want to see perfect examples of how this works just watch a Presidential Press Conference or a White House Briefing (and that goes for both Parties). If the answer to the question asked makes them uncomfortable they simply choose to answer whatever question they would prefer to answer instead, and avoid the difficult question altogether. They stay in their area of experience (or perceived strength).

## *Summary*

Simply put, play to your strengths. Always try to engage your opponent in areas where you are comfortable and confident that you have the advantage. If you play every game on your home field, you're much more likely to end up with a winning record.

Going outside of the experience of your people leads to confusion, fear, retreat, and a lack of communication. Staying in the comfort zone and playing to your strengths allows you to stay on the offensive, and gives you the opportunity to overshadow your weaknesses with your strengths.

## *Rule 3 - Whenever possible go outside the experience of the enemy.*

## Explanation

This tactic is basically a mirror image of the second one. The point of rule three is to find your enemies weaknesses, and spend the majority of your time and effort attacking them there. The best defense is a good offense. You will see this rule played out repeatedly on twitter and virtually everywhere else a Liberal gets a chance to speak.

One of the main ways this rule is used is subject change. If you've ever tried to argue online with a Liberal, particularly a member of Organizing for America, (OFA) formerly Obama for America, then you know that when you are winning the argument the favorite tactic of Liberals is to change the subject. If you've pinned them down on Obama, they'll bring up some obscure issue that they have researched, and you have likely never even heard of. This is no accident. They are trained to do this. When they're losing the argument in an area where you clearly have the upper hand, they simply pull out something that they are likely to know much more about. Whether it's relevant or not is beside the point. Their aim is not really to win a legitimate debate; it is to keep you on the defensive so they can preach their Liberal talking points as long as possible.

If rule two is true, then rule three is obviously true as well. If you are better off playing to your strengths, it is equally true that your opponent will be more vulnerable if you can force them to go outside of their own experience. Like Alinsky, confusing the waiter in the story above, you should always be looking for people who are operating out of habit, and not accustomed to having to deal with changes or questions about what they are doing.

Revisiting football one more time, if you're a good passing team you want to pass as much as possible, but if the opposing team is incompetent at stopping the run, then, by all means, run. Ideally, you can align your strength with your opponents' weakness, but even if you can't you should always be vigilant to see and expose your opponents' weaknesses and force them to go outside of their own area of experience if it can be exploited to your gain.

You will see this often with Liberal commentators on MSNBC and other Left-leaning networks.

# Examples

At the time of this writing (April 2012) the Obama Administration is engaged in a campaign that is based on rules two and three. By introducing social issues during the GOP Primary campaign, they not only seek to show the Republican Party as uncaring, they are also seeking to push the candidates as far Right as they possibly can. Obama's people know that their weakness lies with the losses of support they have suffered among Independents and with female voters.

Their answer - claim that the GOP is engaged in a concerted effort to deny women their reproductive rights. Currently, Liberal mouthpieces are parroting the line, "There is a war on women in the Republican Party". Is it true? It doesn't matter. What matters is the perception they are able to engender. They seem to have successfully moved the argument from a religious freedom issue (should Catholics be forced to provide health care that covers things the Church views as sinful) to an issue of women's productive rights.

The Right, in general, has fumbled this issue because they don't understand Alinsky methods, and if they do, they have no clue how to counter them. The intent of the Obama team is to paint every Republican as an extremist that you can't trust making decisions in Government. This serves the dual purpose of obfuscating the Leftist extremism embraced by President Obama, and forcing the Right to address social issues instead of staying on Obama's abysmal record as President.

By luring GOP candidates into a discussion of women's productive rights, they have effectively changed the subjects. They have taken the public discourse from a discussion of Obama's handling of the economy, Iran, Israel, gas prices, health care, Government intrusion, over regulation, etc. to social issues where they not only poll well, but poll well in a key demographic – namely, women.

If the candidates were savvy, they would just say that they are pro-life, but that they support women's rights to choose what is right for them, and that they believe it is critical that the Government stay out of the business of telling churches what they can do. They should then expose the tactic, and pivot. Don't mention Alinsky, simply say that President Obama is attempting to move the conversation to social issues for shameless political reasons, and that he constantly misstates the position of Republicans on the matter. Furthermore, he is exploiting women with attempts to frighten them into believing that the GOP is somehow going to take away women's rights. All the while, he uses this to obfuscate the real issues of the economy, Government overreaches, and foreign policy; and it is those subjects to which the Republican candidates should pivot. Unfortunately, it doesn't seem that any of the candidates are capable of countering even the most simplistic applications of Alinsky tactics.

### The 2008 Campaign

Barack Obama used each and every rule on this list during the 2008 Presidential campaign. Here are a couple of examples of how he used the third rule:

First, he refused to be drawn out of his area of expertise (although many would claim he has no area of expertise and experience). One of John McCain's greatest strengths has been his performance at "Town Hall" meetings. McCain has excelled in recent years at responding in an impromptu fashion to the questions of voters. Obama, on the other hand, is much more at ease in front of a teleprompter.

Early on in the 2008 Presidential general campaign, McCain challenged Obama to a series of Town Hall events. This was intended to be a challenge in the vein of the Lincoln-Douglas debates, but Obama never even officially acknowledged McCain's challenge. He knew that to do so would be to be lured into the area of his opponent's expertise, and outside of his own. Had McCain continued to hammer the challenge home it is likely that it would have exposed Obama's fear to battle McCain in such a format, but McCain dropped the ball, and allowed Obama to wiggle off the hook. Obama, with the advice of David Axelrod and David Plouffe, was holding fast to rules number two and three, and it paid off. McCain then went on to do only marginally well in the Presidential debates. This only served to reinforce the idea that McCain, while calling for debates, was actually not so skillful in that setting that it would work to his greater good. This, in turn, helped to solidify Obama's position in refusing to debate McCain as McCain had suggested.

Second, was Obama's rather obtuse use of race and his continual plucking at the heartstrings of Americans over a very sordid part of our history. Obama knew that race was his area of experience and expertise, but he was too smart to throw out overt and unsubstantiated claims of racism. Instead, sticking to his area of experience, he took an alternate route to imply that a vote for McCain was not only a vote against Obama, but also a vote against Blacks - and an implied vote for racism.

He used that advantaged position to launch sideswiping attacks like the following comments he made about McCain:

> "He's spending an awful lot of time talking about me. You notice that?" Obama asked a crowd of just over one thousand seated in a university gym. "I haven't seen an ad yet where he talks about what he's going to do. And the reason is because those folks know they don't have any good answers, they know they've had their turn over the last eight years and made a mess of things."

> "They know that you're not real happy with them and so the only way they figure they're going to win this election is if they make you scared of me," Obama continued, repeating an attack from earlier in the day. "What they're saying is 'Well, we know we're not very good but you can't risk electing Obama. You know, he's new, **he doesn't look like the other presidents on the currency, he's a got a funny name**" (emphasis added).[38]

Obama could get away with such overt implications that McCain was somehow racist for two reasons. One, as an African-American, Obama had the right in the minds of most Americans to feel the way he did, because America's history is replete with acts of explicit racism, and scarred by its history of slavery. America is still a place where some obvious racism is seen, and where any black person will agree, America is still a place where subtle racism flourishes.

McCain would have gained a great deal of sympathy had he quoted Obama, and proclaimed with certainty that America was not immune to racism, but that he was no racist, and the great people of America he saw on a daily basis where no racists either. He could then have gone on to exploit any one of a number of Obama weaknesses, but he simply did not. His campaign was mired in a paradigm it thought would succeed, and they held on to it resolutely even when all signs indicated a change was necessary for victory.

Obama succeeded with this tactic not only because of America's guilt over the way African-Americans have been, and are treated, but because it used several of Alinsky's tactics at once. Not only did his comments change the subject to an area in which he was the expert (Rules 2 & 3), but it kept the pressure on the McCain campaign (Rule 10), made the threat seem worse than the reality (Rule 9), and pushed a negative through to a positive (Rule 11).

While it seemed to some that Obama's comments were hurtful and divisive, it was a masterstroke of Alinsky strategy. Incorporating several of the rules at once is an opportunity that is difficult for Alinskyites to resist, and keeping the pressure on your opponent is the central theme of all the tactics. This maneuver worked brilliantly, but it carried within it an inherent risk to Obama. Had anyone in the McCain camp known Alinsky tactics well enough to react properly they could well have done serious damage to Obama with his own words. Interjecting some Jeremiah Wright sermons (something the McCain camp simply ruled out for inexplicable reasons) along with Obama's national address on race, and juxtaposing them with these comments would have been a powerful reply, especially if they were just presented as is, with no comment or judgment by McCain or his campaign.

This was not the only time Obama went to the race card:

> Democratic presidential contender Barack Obama said on Friday he expects Republicans to highlight the fact that he is black as part of an effort to make voters afraid of him.
>
> "It is going to be very difficult for Republicans to run on their stewardship of the economy or their outstanding foreign policy," Obama told a fundraiser in Jacksonville, Florida. "We know what kind of campaign they're going to run. They're going to try to make you afraid.
>
> "They're going to try to make you afraid of me. He's young and inexperienced and he's got a funny name. And did I mention he's black?"[39]

Such attacks allowed Obama to use race against his opponent by staying within an area where he held the advantage and experience. He essentially challenged McCain to enter the arena of race knowing that perceptions would never allow a white man to be seen as a victim of racial politics when he was engaged with an African American. He stayed within his own area of experience and advantage while trying to lure McCain into an area where he would have to fight with a clear disadvantage. This is textbook use of the second and third rules.

Have you ever seen politicians or even business leaders peppered with questions that seem irrelevant? Have you ever been blind-sided in social media by questions and issues with which you know little or nothing? Have you ever seen the mainstream media dwell on seemingly inconsequential issues when covering Conservatives? All of these are textbook examples of the second and third rule. Ignore any strong points made by your opponent, and simply overwhelm him with tangential questions that might exploit some weakness. Even if you never exploit an issue in your favor, you have changed the subject from your weakness, and pushed the momentum of reaction in the direction of your opponent. Now when you see this you won't just chock it up to politics as usual. You will see the puppet master pulling the strings. You will see the man behind the curtain. When you know Alinsky, watching Obama and his team operate suddenly becomes a little like watching The Sixth Sense, and knowing that Bruce Willis' character is dead.

## Summary

As I stated earlier, Rule 3 is just the mirror image of Rule 2. If people operate better when they are doing that with which they are familiar, it follows that people are less capable when asked to outside of their comfort zone. Alinsky's third rule reminds the radical to force his opponent to operate outside of their comfort zone as often as possible. Rules two and three sum up the idea that it is wisest to do what you do best, and attempt to engage your opponent in the things he does most poorly.

# Rule 4 - Make the enemy live up to their own book of rules.

## Explanation

> "The fourth rule is: Make the enemy live up to their own book of rules. You can kill them with this, for they can no more obey their own rules than the Christian church can live up to Christianity."[40]

This tactic too, is genius in its simplicity. The idea is to keep the attention on your opponent by simply peppering them with the ways in which they fail to be perfect. No one is perfect and so the rule is powerful.

In fact, it is one of the most powerful tactics in the Alinsky arsenal. We will see as we go along that this rule, along with the fifth rule and the thirteenth rule are the heart and soul of how the Obama Administration uses Alinsky's rules.

Alinsky singles out the Christian church, because it was through the churches in Chicago that he first began to implement his strategies. When he approached Pastors, he found that it was nearly impossible to speak to them about Christianity (or so he says) because they were focused on the church, the people, the money and all that made up the infrastructure of the institution and not on the philosophy or theology that guided that institution.[41]

Why is this important to understand? It points out a basic flaw. People often profess one thing and then live in complete contradiction to what they profess, or at the very least neglect, the things that they claim are most important in favor of what they find most expedient. In politics, the fact that politicians say one thing and do another has become cliché. Don't sleep on this one. It is legitimate to hold people accountable for the promises they make.

Clearly, people being people are generally going to fall short of any expectations they put upon themselves. The key Alinsky found was that this could be used to discredit a person or entity that professed one system of morality, but lived by another. It is a deceptively simple and powerful tactic, and it is one tactic that the Right has allowed the Left to own without a fight.

For a Conservative, the standard seems much higher because they embrace the mantle of religiosity and morality, but should this allow the Left free reign to behave as they please simply because they never claimed the moral high ground? Surely, the person professing morality would be more susceptible to an attack of hypocrisy, but when someone on the Left does something morally abhorrent or flat out illegal, should they be held unaccountable? Make both sides live up to their promises. If they don't, beat them over the head with it relentlessly.

A morally bankrupt act or a broken promise is fair game for both sides. Why is it that those on the Left are the only ones to hit their opponents over the head with inconsistencies? We will have more on this in the chapter on defeating the Alinsky tactics.

For example, suppose someone you know is encouraging you to stop smoking (oh, I don't know let's just say it's the President of the United States), because they assure you that they are concerned about your health. They know the dangers of tobacco and they care about you. You really need to stop smoking so you can be around to be their friend.

Now let's suppose you find out that this person (oh, I don't know let's just say it's the President of the United States again) is actually smoking themselves. The next time they tell you that you need to quit smoking, what is the first thing you're going to say? You are going to say, "Hey, wait a minute. Don't lecture me about smoking when I happen to know you do it yourself". You would be telling them to live up to their own book or rules - this is Alinsky's fourth rule, and is a strategy against which it is difficult to defend.

# Examples

In an article entitled, "I still hate you, Sarah Palin" David Kahane of the National Review Online lays out how Obama eviscerated Palin with *Rules for Radicals* and finishes by saying this,

> "What you clowns need, in other words, is a Rules for Radical Conservatives to explain what you're up against and teach you how to compete before it's too late."[42]

In essence, what I am presenting here is just such a manual for Conservatives, but with a twist. Yes, I am aware that other books exist on this subject, but just because I was remiss in publishing my book in a timely manner does not mean that it doesn't add a unique perspective. I believe this book lays things out in a clear manner, and offers plain explanations and practical advice that you will not find anywhere else, and even more importantly, this book offers a way to beat them without completely joining them. You will learn how to counter tactics, not just how to use them. While Conservatives are beginning to come around to what *Rules for Radicals* is all about, I have been screaming about it for way too long now, and the dates on many of my Blog posts precede any of the other books on this subject.

Now, back to the matter at hand -They destroyed Palin, or "*Palinized*" her, because she was too nice to fight back using their own tactics, or because the McCain's handlers held her back. I don't think she'd make that same mistake again. In fact, there were signs towards the end of the campaign that her "going rogue" was about finally fighting back. Remember, "Paling around with terrorists"? Since 2008, Sarah Palin has come a long way in "going rogue". While I admire her willingness to punch back, she would do well, in my opinion, to let the media be the media and stay on subject.

An important point to consider: one does not need to sink fully to the levels of Alinsky style tactics to defeat them. Sometimes, yes. Sometimes, no. Knowing how to spot them, how to counteract them, and when to use them and when not to use them is the key to beating this insidious political methodology. You'll see me repeat this often, because it is important, "The action is in the reaction".

The author of the above article concluded that Palin was just too nice. The result was that she was destroyed by rule four. Her pregnant daughter, Bristol was perhaps the best example. Constantly harping on the fact that Palin believed in abstinence, while she had a daughter who was pregnant out of wedlock was one issue that helped the Obama campaign to beat her over the head with her own book of rules.

At the same time, Obama was telling everyone that his family was off limits. In fact, he feigned sympathy for Palin's family. All this happened while Axelrod, Plouffe and the rest of the Obama hit squad were finding every way possible to trash Palin and her family. Obama did what he always does – he distanced himself from the despicable attacks by using his proxies. All the while, however, we know full well that none of it was happening without the approval of Obama. Challenge me on this one if you would like to Mr. President.

This rule is a favorite of the Left. They relish the opportunity to attack anyone who claims to live a moral life. In essence, they have created an environment in which it is preferable simply to say you have no moral code rather than aspire to morality and fail.

Does the phrase, "Read my lips, no new taxes" ring a bell? When George H.W. Bush uttered those words, and then went on to raise taxes, he defeated himself. All that Bill Clinton (remember his wife's connection to Alinsky) had to do was to hammer Bush over the head with this inconsistency. It worked.

This rule also helps Alinskyites like Barack Obama to remember to read every word of the rules. When he first sought office in Chicago, he was able to eliminate his competition by using arcane rules to disqualify sufficient numbers of signators from qualifying to sign his opponent's list of potential voters. Likewise, it was Obama's familiarity with the minutest details of the nomination process that helped defeat Hillary Clinton in the 2008 Primary.[43]

The most powerful use of Alinsky's fourth rule by the 2008 Obama campaign came when he did everything in his power to merge John McCain with George W. Bush. He went so far as to say that electing John McCain would be tantamount to giving George W. Bush a third term. He continually portrayed McCain as part of the status quo, and part of those in Washington who simply wanted to engage in politics as usual. On the other hand, Obama presented himself as the agent of change. After all, "Hope and Change" was the mantra that accompanied Obama's Presidential campaign.

In one of Obama's 2008 campaign spots an announcer says in response to McCain's line, "Senator Obama, I am not President Bush": "True, but you did vote with Bush 90% of the time. Tax breaks for big corporations and the wealthy, but almost nothing for the middle class – same as Bush."

Obama constantly asserted that McCain would continue George W. Bush's policies.[44]

By tying McCain to Bush, he could then use anything that he used against Bush against McCain. Now, it became a simple matter for Obama to use the unpopularity of Bush as a millstone around McCain's neck. He proceeded to not only make McCain live up to his own book or rules, but he also required McCain to live up to George W. Bush's book of rules.

This tactic is quite common. After his election, Obama began to refer to the GOP as the "Party of no". Obama agglomerated all Republicans together under one negative, umbrella term, and thereby marginalized members of the minority Party until the election of 2010.

In a move, I believe to be unprecedented by a sitting President, Obama and his advisers decided to attack a radio talk show host. The Obama people, particularly David Axelrod, began to refer to Rush Limbaugh as the de facto head of the Republican Party. While this is a genius move for reasons I will explain; it is a tactic that most would consider below the dignity of the office of the President of the United States.

Why was it such a genius move to make Rush Limbaugh the de facto head of the Republican Party? There are two reasons why this was a smart move even though it doesn't seem like one on the surface. First, it allowed the Obama team and Democrats in general, to attack any and all Republicans with everything Rush Limbaugh was saying, or had ever said. This enabled the Dems to dig up every controversial remark Limbaugh ever made (and there are a lot of them), and force any given Republican to defend those remarks. Second, Rush Limbaugh is known for fighting back, even against members of the Republican Party. This put the Democrats in the delightful position of pointing out ridiculous statements by Limbaugh, and forcing random Republicans to defend these statements - knowing full well that if they disagree with Limbaugh they will be hearing their names on his popular radio program.

Limbaugh's ego combined with his large audience proved to be the perfect breeding ground for the Left. As soon as

Limbaugh said something that polled badly, the Left jumped on it and began to ask any Republican available if they agreed with Rush. Since so many in the media lean heavily Left, and are a part of a certain groupthink, they were complicit with the tactic.

We'll discuss how easily such tactics can be countered later, but for now, we are satisfied simply to show how the tactics are used. Examples like these can go on and on, but the point is simply to make the reader understand the tactics here, and so we move to tactic five.

## Summary

This is perhaps the most underutilized tool available to Conservatives, but for some reason they seem loathe to use it. Making the enemy live up to their own book of rules can be as simple as calling attention to what people have said in comparison to what they have done. Alternatively, it can be used more broadly. Holding people to the very highest ideals to which they subscribe may seem to some a bridge too far, but don't be surprised if those using the Alinsky model do exactly that.

# Rule 5 - Ridicule is man's most potent weapon.

## Explanation

> The fourth rule carries within it the fifth rule: Ridicule is man's most potent weapon. It is almost impossible to counterattack ridicule. Also, it infuriates the opposition, who then react to your advantage.[45]

It hardly seems necessary to explain what ridicule is. Much like the Supreme Court with obscenity, we know it when we see it. Dictionary.com defines ridicule as,

> speech or action intended to cause contemptuous laughter at a person or thing; derision.[46]

The fifth rule is perhaps the most used, and thus overused of the 13 tactics. It is also the first in this list that makes most of us a bit uneasy. We have been taught since childhood that it is not right to make fun of people, and most people's moral center rebels at the idea of embracing such a tactic. If we believe, as does Alinsky, that the end justifies the means then we have no such repulsion at using rules, which seek to exploit, our baser instincts. However, we must not turn a blind eye while the Alinskyites use this rule against us.

It strikes me as odd, the amount of enjoyment Alinsky seems to take from this tactic. He says later in the chapter,

> It should be remembered that you can threaten the enemy and get away with it. You

> can insult and annoy him, but the one thing
> that is unforgivable and that is certain to get
> him to react is to laugh at him. This causes an
> irrational anger.[47]

Notice, if you will, a few things about the way Alinsky describes this rule. First, he says that if follows from the fourth. You'll recall that the fourth rule was to make the enemy live up to their own book of rules. The implication then is that when your opponent fails to live up to his own book of rules, he opens himself up to rightful derision. The Left has been using this one-two punch against Conservatives for years now. As the Right claims the moral high ground, the Left need only wait for the first sight of human frailty, and pounce on it with the vigor of a lion upon its prey. The Left seems to feel that by holding to no morality, they are then exempt from the derision heaped upon those who fall short of their moral code.

Secondly, Alinsky says that it is almost impossible to counterattack ridicule. He is correct, but only insofar as the word "almost" remains. If you don't believe that it is nearly impossible to overcome ridicule, just look what the Left and a complicit Left-leaning media did to Sarah Palin. Once the ridicule started, the momentum was too great to stop by election time. Liberals frequently do this same thing, especially when they have no real facts upon which to base their arguments.

You should never be surprised when a Liberal calls a Conservative racist or stupid. This is their go-to move. If they can mock you, they have no need to come up with a cogent argument for their point. I have often posed the question, "How can you tell when a Liberal is dead?" The answer: They stop calling you a racist. Another famous tweet of mine is apropos here – "Calling people racist – it's the Liberal "get out of logic free card".

Thirdly, there is this recurrent theme of action and reaction. Remember, this is the real key to understanding and defeating Alinsky tactics. Alinsky says that ridicule leads to infuriation, which leads to a reaction that can be used against your opponent. The subject of action and reaction is central to the efficacy of the Alinsky Model.

# Examples

If you want to understand the role that ridicule plays in the Alinsky method, and particularly in the way in which the Obama Administration uses Alinsky, you need look no further than Sarah Palin. From the moment that she was introduced as John McCain's running mate the Alinsky machine within Obama's campaign flew into action at full speed to find ways to mock, denigrate, and ridicule her. Obama's campaign dispatched a slew of vultures to descend on Alaska in an effort to dig dirt, stir trouble, and uncover any malcontent who might have the tiniest bit of salacious information on the Governor.

Perhaps nothing so typified the mockery of Palin as Saturday Night Lives' treatment of the Alaska Governor. To this day, many people still believe that Sarah Palin said that she could see Russia from her house. Sorry to disappoint the Left on this one, but it was Tina Fey as Sarah Palin that uttered those words. It is unfortunately not that uncommon for people to take Saturday Night Live or the John Stewart show as real news. The Left is fond of claiming Conservatives are stupid, ill informed, and lacking in nuance, yet the Left is constantly citing sources such as Jon Stewart as though his program is actual news.

However, it was not just the comedians that perpetrated the misinformation and ridicule of the Alaska Governor. The mainstream media, joined at the hip with the "historic" Obama campaign, went to great lengths in their complicity to mock and discredit Sarah Palin. The *Palinization* continues to this day. After her appearance at the Tea Party convention her "poor man's teleprompter" i.e. the notes scribbled on her hand were mocked incessantly by everyone up to and including White House spokesperson Robert Gibbs. Obama's introduction of himself through teleprompter malfunction seems to have eluded the media coverage.

As adults, we don't typically think of ridicule as an effective means of getting what we want. This type of behavior is usually seen as immature. It reminds most of us of a time when all insults were rubber, and their perpetrators glue. However, ridicule has emerged as an extremely powerful political tool.

In 2006, then Senator Obama visited Kenya to assist the campaign of his cousin Raila Odinga. Among the issues embraced by Odinga's Party was this, taken from one of their leaked documents,

> "The age issue: Our core supporters are essentially young people who are angry about the domination of Kibaki politics by frail septuagenarians. "

> Billboards and leaflets ridiculing the old people in the Kibaki team were in contrast this with the billboards of Hon Raila, which featured young people as, "the promise of a buoyant future."[48]

Is it mere coincidence then that during the 2008 campaign, the Obama people released a television spot claiming that John McCain "admits he still can't use a computer"? The narrator says,

> "1982, John McCain goes to Washington. Things have changed in the last 26 years, but McCain hasn't. He admits he still doesn't know how to use a computer, can't send an e-mail, still doesn't understand the economy, and favors 200 billion in new tax cuts for corporations, but almost nothing for the middle class. After one president who was out of touch, we just can't afford more of the same."[49]

The idea was to paint McCain as out of touch (read "old"), while Obama was the cool new candidate who really "got" the younger generation. Unfortunately, the Obama ad was not only inaccurate; it was derogatory towards a war hero. McCain did indeed once admit that he had trouble using a computer, but as ABCNews.com puts it,

> McCain did once describe himself as computer "illiterate" and dependent upon his wife for computer assistance, but there's more to the tale than that.

> Assuredly McCain isn't comfortable talking about this — and the McCain campaign discouraged me from writing about this — but the reason the aged Arizonan doesn't use a

> computer or send e-mail is because of his war
> wounds.[50]

Now, that is the type of ridicule the Obama camp stooped to in 2008, and they didn't stop there. The ad actually mocks anyone who isn't as tech savvy as the younger generation. Odd, since Obama himself had a twitter account for months before informing the world that he had never tweeted.[51]

Even as President, Obama has not hesitated to use ridicule. During the months leading up to the 2010-midterm elections the President repeatedly referred to the Republican Party as having driven the economy into the ditch, and instead of helping to get the car out they were haranguing the Democrats. He even went so far as to say that the Republicans were up on the road drinking slurpees and complaining while the Democrats were working arduously to get the economy back on the road.[52]

Adding insult to insult, the President went on to say,

> [W]e can't have special interests sitting shotgun. We gotta have middle class families up in front. [Cheers and applause.] We can't, uh— We don't mind the Republicans joining us. They can come for the ride, but they gotta sit in back. [53]

In 2012, after embracing the "all of the above" energy policy he sneered at during the 2008 campaign, Obama proceeded to mock the Republican Party for wanting to do more domestic drilling of oil. In an address to his supporters he said,

Let me tell you something. If some of these folks were around when Columbus set sail—[Laughter]—they must have been founding members of the Flat Earth Society [Laughter]. They would not have believed that the world was round [Applause]. We've heard these folks in the past. They probably would have agreed with one of the pioneers of the radio who said, 'Television won't last. It's a flash in the pan' [Laughter]. One of Henry Ford's advisers was quoted as saying, 'The horse is here to stay but the automobile is only a fad' [Laughter].' [35]

The President and his advisers are so fond of rule five that it is difficult to find a stopping point, but for clarity and space, I will stop here assuming that you get the idea, and see the President's predilection for using ridicule in a manner that exceeds any of his predecessors. His fondness for ridicule makes many of us feel that it demeans the nobility of the office he holds.

## A Few Practical Guidelines for Using Ridicule

Never use ridicule to attack innocent people such as the family of the person you are opposing.

Never use ridicule that includes racism, sexism, or homophobia.
It is always preferable to use ridicule that includes humor.

Never allow yourself to be provoked into ridicule. It should only be used as a well thought out plan.

When you want to use ridicule, ask yourself if there is another way to do it - if there is – you should probably do it the other way.

Let your conscience be your guide, but make sure you are honest with yourself about whether you are violating your own moral code.

Don't fall in love with this tactic. It can be effective, but it can easily lead you to being like the very people you are opposing.

## Summary

Ridicule is a favorite of the Obama camp just as it was a favorite of Alinsky. Alinsky's biographer says,

> Alinsky was especially captivated by Lewis's flair for rhetorically skewering political opponents. Lewis's attitude seemed to be that there was no fun or skill in merely waylaying an adversary; one had to use some imagination. On one occasion, Alinsky told Hyman that Lewis had used a word he had never heard before to ridicule an opponent, a word Alinksy obviously planned to add to his own arsenal. What was the word? Hyman asked. "Retromingian," Alinsky said with a mischievous grin, setting u Hyman's inevitable question. "You're going to call some guy a retromingian," Human said. "What in the hell is that?" And Alinsky replied: "It's a kind of dumb animal that urinates backwards."[54]

Alinskyite's really enjoy this stuff. The "thrill up the leg" comes when they can really denigrate someone to a subhuman level. While I believe some ridicule is useful – tread lightly lest in trying to defeat them – you become them.

## *Rule 6 - A good tactic is one that your people enjoy.*

## Explanation

> The sixth rule is: A good tactic is one that your people enjoy. If your people are not having a ball doing it, there is something very wrong with the tactic.[55]

This tactic too seems rather self-explanatory. Happy, enthusiastic people do a better job than people who are merely going through the motions, or people whose zeal has waned. If you expect excellence, it is critical that people enjoy what they're doing. The concept that a happy workplace is a more productive one is not new, but like most clichés, neither is it false. Moreover, in politics the veracity of the cliché holds more than ever – morale matters.

Given that they have been using the same tactics for nearly five years now, you can well expect the Democrats to make some dramatic turns in their approach between now and November of 2012. In a later chapter, I will attempt to make some predictions about what the Left might try during the Presidential campaign of 2012, and I hope to help you to see some of what's coming before it arrives.

# Examples

Before we proceed, you need to know a little bit about Obama for America (OFA). During the 2008 Presidential campaign, the Obama Administration used their knowledge of community organizing to create an entity called Organizing for America. This was a group of "paid volunteers", composed mainly of young people, particularly those most capable of harnessing the power of the Internet and social networking to benefit Mr. Obama.

They did things like making calls for Obama, initiating flash mobs to make it seem as though the public was more interested in a particular event than it actually was, commenting positively for Obama on popular articles, and promoting Obama and his ideas on social networks like Facebook and twitter. Social media is likely to have a much larger impact in 2012 than it did in 2008. Fortunately, Conservative have become adept at Social media However, it will take morale at least as high as that displayed by Conservatives in 2010 to remove Barack Obama from office.

In any case, this group of "paid volunteers" did Obama's bidding up to and including texting their supporters with reminders to vote. The other side of the coin found these same OFA workers simultaneously destroying Hillary Clinton, John McCain, and Sarah Palin in as raunchy and vicious a manner as possible. When Obama won election, he could no longer technically keep his campaign staff on as paid members of his Administration so in true Obama manner he simply changed the name of the group from *Organizing for America* to *Obama for America*, and changed their description to an advocacy group.

I bring up the OFA at this point for several reasons. First, these are the Obama Administration worker bees. They are the ones that Alinsky would say, "should be having a ball" at what they do. To that end, Obama's "Alinsky savvy" handlers gave their acolytes some ways to have fun promoting the Obama agenda.

If you're a Conservative on twitter and you speak your mind you have already, no doubt, had some run-ins with OFA. They troll twitter and Facebook for terms that might clue them in to the fact that someone is speaking out against Obama or one of his policies. When they find you, they often descend en masse to level all manner of false accusations against you, and call you every name they can think of.

In the fall of 2009, I began a hashtag on twitter with some help from some very wonderful people, including my co-founder Ron Dickerhoof (@RDickerhoof). The hashtag (#OCRA) is still going strong. In case you're wondering, it stands for Organized Conservative Resistance Alliance, and you can read more about it on my blog at http://www.AlinskyDefeater.com/Blog/. I mention the hashtag only because during the first few nights of its existence, my friends and I were met with an onslaught of opposition from OFA and other Liberals who took great pleasure in calling us everything but nice people.

It has been my observation over the past three years that the Obama people have kept their OFA clones happy doing their job by encouraging them to do things like call people racists, talk down to people and call them stupid, and claiming that they have the market on compassion cornered. OFA has been given some other "treats" like attacking Rush Limbaugh, Glenn Beck, and Andrew Breitbart (RIP), but mostly they have just been allowed to troll for Conservatives and use Alinsky tactics against them. By using Alinsky tactics, they are frequently able to get Conservatives off message or make them so angry that they do their cause a disservice in the way they respond.

If you find me repeating something, it's not an accident. The action is in the reaction!

## Summary

It seems obvious that morale is important, but if you remember the sparse crowds and lack of enthusiasm following GOP nominee John McCain in 2008 before he selected Sarah Palin as his running mate, then you know that is not a subject that should be ignored. The Obama Administration seems to keep its acolytes happy by constantly giving them ever more salacious tactics to exploit. The trick for the Right is to harness the enthusiasm that it had in 2010. Right now, – I don't see it – and it worries me a great deal.

## Rule 7 - A tactic that drags on too long becomes a drag.

## Explanation

> The seventh rule: A tactic that drags on too long becomes a drag. Man can sustain militant interest in any issue for only a limited time, after which it becomes a ritualistic commitment, like going to church on Sunday mornings. New issues and crises are always developing, and one's reaction becomes, "Well, my heart bleeds for those people and I'm all for the boycott, but after all there are other important things in life" – and there it goes.[56]

People get bored when they are called upon to do things repeatedly without change. While Obama clearly captured the enthusiasm of a large sector of the population in 2008, keeping that enthusiasm among the very people who had to hear the same speeches repeated, and who were forced to use the same arguments to fight for their candidate was another matter altogether. This is where the transition from *Organizing for America* to *Obama for America* became so crucial.

The seventh rule is just an extension of the sixth rule. Even tactics that people enjoy can become stale. It is the job of the community organizer to constantly update the strategies in a way that keep the people excited about what they are doing.

# Examples

How many times can you call the Republican Party the Party of no? How many times can you blame George Bush? How many times can you call your opposition racists for disagreeing with you? How many times can you claim all Conservatives are stupid? How many times can you claim the Tea Party is violent, with no evidence to back it up? How many times can you say the economy is like a car in a ditch and the Republicans are drinking slurpees instead of helping get it out?

At first blush, based upon the record of the Obama Administration and its defenders over the course of his first three years in office the answer would seem to be a very large number indeed. Such questions cannot keep OFA or any of Obama's hatchet men enthused indefinitely, however. Eventually, the people defending you will tire of the same threadworm arguments being regurgitated ad nauseam.

In other words, if you want to keep the dogs happy and ready to attack on command, it behooves you to throw them some fresh meat from time to time. People may genuinely believe, to their very core, every single principle for which you stand, but if they are forced to defend those principles, using the same tactics over and over again their enthusiasm will eventually wane. Remember, Alinsky says,

> A good tactic is one that your people enjoy. If your people are not having a ball doing it, there is something very wrong with the tactic.[57]

Keeping OFA and the rest of Obama's supporters enthusiastic is a critical element for the Obama team, and so you can expect any number of additional attack lines from them by this fall. I would not be surprised, however, if the Left is still blaming George W. Bush, and claiming there is a racist behind every tree.

## Summary

Even the best tactic can grow old over time. It is important to keep people engaged and enthusiastic by providing them with new and entertaining strategies.

## *Rule 8 - Keep the pressure on with different tactics, and actions, and utilize all events of the period for your purpose.*

## Explanation

> The eighth rule: Keep the pressure on, with different tactics and actions, and utilize all events of the period for your purpose.[58]

Most people who know anything about Saul Alinsky and *Rules for Radicals* are familiar with rules five and thirteen. Those two tactics have garnered more press than all the other rules combined, but it is rule eight that best encapsulates the central thesis of the Alinsky model. The Alinsky mode is all about pressure. Remember, "The action is in the reaction." In rule 10, we will take this even a step further to describe what I like to refer to as the Alinsky reaction chain. Do you recall what I said about things I repeat? *The action is in the reaction* and the way to produce reactions is keep the pressure on.

The genius of Alinsky is in his understanding what is necessary to motivate people to organize, his gift for finding creative ways to use these motivated people to apply the right kind of pressure on the people in power. Although he claims his goal is to heal society and bring about fairness, it is clear that his immediate goal is to "rub raw the resentments of the people" until they are so dissatisfied with their lot in life that they will rise up against the "Haves", topple them from power, and rebuild a new, fairer society in its place. If all this talk of revolutions, Haves, Have-nots, and building a new, fairer society remind you of Karl Marx – you are not alone.

Alinsky purposely chose not to self identify, but in *Let Them Call Me Rebel*, Horwitt says,

> Alinsky had no formal affiliation with the Communist Party, but liked to think of himself as "emotionally aligned very strongly with it". [59]

So, Alinsky never claimed to be a Marxist or a Communist, but the pages of his books drip with Marxist terminology. As Horwitt shows, this is not a coincidence.

In the *Communist Manifesto* Marx and Engels say,

> The proletarian movement is the self-conscious, independent movement of the immense majority, in the interest of the

immense majority. The proletariat, the lowest stratum of our present society, cannot stir, cannot raise itself up, without the whole superincumbent strata of official society being sprung into the air.[60]

Marx and Alinsky differ in their vision of how capitalism would ultimately fall. Marx saw it as inevitably a violent overthrow of the proletariat (the 'haves') by the bourgeoisie (the 'have-nots') while Alinsky envisioned a peaceful, albeit chaotic, transition from capitalism to some brand of Utopian Socialism. Both men however, embraced the idea that the key to the inescapable collapse of capitalism required organizing the 'have-nots' because their sheer numbers empower them if they work in concert. This is the fundamental premise of community organization. Ironically, it is also the very reason that President Obama cannot enact his entire agenda. Without the support of the bourgeois, he lacks the political power. Instead, he now becomes just another person trying to champion the minority; a methodology that has been used with varying degrees of success, but which both Marx and Alinsky would agree are wholly unable to achieve the ultimate ends of toppling the status quo.

Before we continue to dissect the eighth rule, carefully consider each of the following Alinsky quotes:

> *The real action is in the enemy's reaction.*
>
> *The enemy, properly goaded and guided in his reaction, will be your major strength.*

*Tactics, like organization, like life, require that you move with the tactics.*

*In the beginning, the organizer's first job is to create the issues or problems.*

*The first step in community organization is community disorganization.*

*This is why the organizer...must first rub raw the resentments of the people of the community.*

*He [the community organizer] must search out controversy.*

*When those prominent in the status quo turn and label you an "agitator" they are completely correct, for that is, in one word, your function – to agitate to the point of conflict.*

*Action comes from keeping the heat on.*

## Examples

Specifically, Alinsky mentions three ways in rule eight to keep the pressure on the opposition:

1. Use different tactics
2. Use different actions
3. Utilize all events of the period for your purpose.

## Different Tactics

In *Rules for Radicals* Alinsky says,

> There can be no prescriptions for particular situations because the same situation rarely recurs, any more than history repeats itself. People, pressures, and patterns of power are variables, and a particular combination exists only in a particular time -even then the variables are constantly in a state of flux.[61]

Alinsky was aware that most would-be community organizers simply did not have the ability to see the larger picture. They lacked the imagination to vary their tactics in accordance with overriding principles, but instead clung to verbatim applications of Alinsky's tactics. Alinsky says of these unsuccessful community organizers,

> I hesitate to spell out specific applications of these tactics. I remember an unfortunate experience with my *Reveille for Radicals*, in which I collected accounts of particular actions and tactics employed in organizing a number of communities. For some time after the book was published I got reports that would-be organizers were using this book as a manual, and whenever they were confronted with a puzzling situation they would retreat into some vestibule or alley and thumb through to find the answer![43]

Alinsky never envisioned his work as a cookie cutter approach to change. Instead, it was meant to provide a framework upon which creative individuals could build successful methodologies to invert the power structure in America. You cannot simply read and learn the Alinsky tactics, and then call upon them in rote fashion to meet the needs of each situation as it arises. Alinsky posits that community organizing is more an art form than a science. While there are certain principles that hold true, the application of those principles to specific scenarios requires a certain mental agility that not all possess.

The architects of the Obama campaign and Administration have proven to be quite adept at applying Alinsky tactics in an artful and flexible manner. His chief advisors, David Plouffe, David Axelrod, and Valerie Jarrett have all demonstrated the ability to adapt to very different circumstances with creative applications of Alinsky's overriding principles. Without such deviceful methods of extensibility, the Affordable Care Act (a.k.a. Obamacare) would never have been pushed through Congress. In fact, Obamacare is an excellent example of how the nimble and creative use of Alinsky tactics can succeed where a more rigid approach would surely fail.

The ability on the part of the Obama Administration to apply differing tactics to seemingly implacable problems proved to be the key to the passage of Obamacare. From its inception, the Affordable Care Act was met with a high level of intransigent opposition on both sides of the aisle. Like Hillary-care before it, it seemed dead in the water on several occasions. The ability of Obama and his advisors to continue to think on their feet, and relentlessly push Obamacare with differing tactics finally proved successful.

Consider some of the adjustments necessary on the part of the Obama team for the final passage of Obamacare.

Initially, it was pushed as the "right of every American", but as the public objected (especially in the town hall meetings held by members of Congress in the fall of 2009) Obama and company adjusted their tactics. The next step was a litany of sob stories, some of which were provably fabricated, to tug at the sympathies of a fundamentally compassionate American electorate. Obama also used 'plants'[62] in his health care town hall meetings to push his agenda. Most of us would find the intentional deception of fellow Americans morally repugnant, and would never consider planting people in audiences at health care town halls with fake stories to push a political agenda in spite of its massive unpopularity. However, with Alinsky as their guide, the means were irrelevant if the end would be what they perceived of as the greater good for America.

Such hubris reminds us of Alinsky's words,

> But it is equally difficult for you to surrender that little image of God created in our own likeness, which lurks in all of us and tells us that we secretly believe that we know what's best for the people.

And again,

> The ego of the organizer is stronger and more monumental than the ego of the leader. The leader is driven by the desire for power, while the organizer is driven by the desire to create. The organizer is in a true sense reaching for the highest level for which man can reach – to create, to be a "great creator," to play God.[63]

I would argue that creativity may well be one of man's highest callings, but to usurp the role of the great creator is man's lowest calling – a calling which echoes that of Satan himself whose crime was to attempt to "play God". This is just more of Alinsky's convoluted moral relativism mixed with his naïve understanding of dualism.

Even such extreme tactics by the President proved inadequate to get Obamacare through Congress, and so they again adjusted tactics. After offering every backroom deal possible and still falling short of the requisite votes and with Senate Majority Leader Harry Reid clinging to the notion that reconciliation would never be used to pass The Affordable Care Act, things seemed bleak for team Obama. Additionally, the untimely death of Senator Kennedy and the surprising election of Republican Scott Brown as his replacement in Massachusetts seemed to sound the death knell for Obamacare, but the community-organizer-in-chief would not be denied so easily. Instead, Obama's team made yet another course correction. With little fanfare, the Democrats and their Majority Leader in the Senate had an epiphany, and out of the blue reconciliation was now considered an acceptable and commonly used practice; a practice that would be completely acceptable as a means to transfer 1/6 of the American economy out of private hands and into the hands of unelected bureaucrats.

Obama's refusal to take no for an answer - either from Congress or from the American people - demonstrates the Alinsky method. When you are so convinced that you know what's best for people even when they don't want it, you become relentless in pursuit of your desired end. Obama's willingness to change tactics on the fly illustrates perfectly the way Alinsky teaches his followers to keep the pressure on with different tactics.

## *Different Actions*

The second part of Alinsky's method of maintaining consistent pressure on the opposition is to use different actions. While different actions are not vastly different from different tactics, there is a nuanced difference. Tactics are the ideas while actions are the implementation of those ideas.

As Alinsky said,

> Among the organizers I trained and failed with, there were some who memorized the words and the related experiences and concepts. Listening to them was like listening to a tape playing back my presentation word for word. Clearly, there was little understanding; clearly, they could not do more than elementary organization. The problem with so many of them was and is their failure to understand that a statement of a specific situation is significant only in its relationship to and its illumination of a general concept. Instead, they see the specific action as a terminal point. They find it difficult to grasp the fact that no situation ever repeats itself, that no tactic can be precisely the same.[64]

They see the specific action as a terminal point. In other words, Alinsky felt that would-be community organizers fell too easily into a pattern of enacting tactics in the same tired, unimaginative, and overused ways. Where marching in the street might be the best approach in one set of circumstances, different circumstances could just as easily call for a very different approach. By way of example, Alinsky cites an instance in which he intended to gather 'a hundred blacks' to create havoc at a symphony concert. His plan was to feed them a large meal of baked beans before the concert, and have them enter the hall en masse. He recounts that the concert had many quiet moments and the results would be predictable, and effective at creating a disturbance without a mass meeting, march in the streets, or picketing outside the building. Alinsky concludes his story by saying, "Imagine the scene when the action began! The concert would be over before the first movement! (If this be a Freudian slip-so be it!)"[65]

It is in the implementation of tactics that the community organizer must be most creative. Alinsky prided himself in seeing ways to make his points in creative and thought provoking ways that others simply did not see. It is in this area that it becomes difficult to teach Alinsky tactics. Without the ability to think about situations in creative ways, you cannot truly be successful with Alinsky tactics. It is certain however, that you cannot use the tactics in creative ways if you do not first learn them thoroughly.

How successful you will be at defeating Alinsky tactics or at using them yourself is a product of your willingness to learn the general principles completely combined with your ability to use that knowledge with your creativity to act in ways that will throw your opponent off. You can learn to recognize and expose Alinsky tactics by learning the over-arching principles, but the level of success you will have at implementing them will still be dependent upon your ability to use them in highly nuanced and creative ways. If you are to master the tactics, you must be as the highly trained athlete who constantly works to reinforce his mastery of the fundamentals, but who also realizes that to play the game at the highest levels he or she has to reach "a zone" where creativity and fundamentals merge as one.

As Alinsky said,

> Tactics must be understood as specific applications of the rules and principles that I have listed above. It is the principles that the organizer must carry with him in battle. To these he applies his imagination, and he relates them tactically to specific situations.[66]

## *Utilize all events of the period for your purpose*

Who can forget these words of President Obama's then Chief of Staff, Rahm Emanuel?

> "You never want a serious crisis to go to waste. And what I mean by that is an opportunity to do things you think you could not do before."[67]

Emmanuel was speaking of the financial crisis of 2008 – 2009, and how Barack Obama and the Democrats would be able to seek to capitalize politically. He was laying the groundwork for Americans to accept the "fundamental transformation of America" that the new President was about to undertake in his first days in office. To most Americans those words seemed oddly out of place. It seemed unseemly and almost un-American to refer to a catastrophe as an opportunity to push a political agenda. The scope and severity of the global financial crises seemed an inappropriate backdrop for political gamesmanship, and yet to those who understand Alinsky it seemed not only apposite, but also somehow predictable.

The Obama Administration has shown a remarkable level of skill at utilizing the events of the period for their purposes. The financial crisis was an excuse for a nearly $1 trillion 'stimulus' that by most accounts provided very little by way of actual stimulus. It did however; provide huge sums of money to state and local municipalities, complete with strings attached to increase the Federal Government's level of control. It also served to pay back many of Obama's supporters for their generous contributions to his successful Presidential bid.

The global financial crisis was not the only event appropriated by the White House for political purposes. In fact, when no actual crisis exists you can always manufacture one, and this is precisely what they did with Obamacare. While most would agree that health care in America was in need of a serious overhaul, the change brought about by Obamacare was more about consolidation of power in the Federal Government than truly reducing costs and providing care for more people. As previously stated, stories abounded that were meant to tug at the heartstrings of Americans. Many of those stories were invented out of whole cloth. For a quick look at some of those plants in Obama town hall meetings WND has a nice piece at http://www.wnd.com/2009/08/1 06811/.

The BP oil spill provided yet another crisis to exploit. Here was the perfect opportunity for the Obama Administration to shut down drilling in the Gulf of Mexico in an effort to reinforce their "green agenda". Likewise, Climate Change provided the cover necessary to allow the Obama Administration to pick winners and losers in the market even as the financial crisis afforded them the ability to pick winners and losers in the financial industry and even in the automotive industry. We could go on, but you get the point. This Administration has moved adroitly to capitalize on every available circumstance to promote their agenda. The next crisis or war that America faces, you will now be forewarned to watch for the political maneuverings as Obama seeks to promote his far-Left agenda with his skillful use of Alinsky tactics. You can count on Obama and his advisors to "Keep the pressure on, with different tactics and actions, and utilize all events of the period for [their] purpose."

## *Summary*

Pressure, pressure, pressure; with the Alinsky model, success is all about the pressure. Remember, the action is in the reaction. Constant pressure causes people to make mistakes, which you can then capitalize on by applying even more pressure, and so it goes. In the eighth rule, Alinsky mentions three ways to keep the pressure on your opponent:

1. Use different tactics (strategies)

2. Use different actions (application of strategies)

3. Utilize all events of the period for your purpose (exploit anything – good, bad, or horrific for your own political gain)

# Rule 9 - The threat is usually more terrifying than the thing itself.

## Explanation

The ninth rule is

> The threat is usually more terrifying than the thing itself.[68]

The ninth rule is rather simple and self-explanatory. In fact, it is the only rule of the thirteen listed by Alinsky in **Rules for Radicals** that does not include any further exposition by the author. However, don't let this fool you. It is critical to recognize this rule, and know how to respond when it is used against you. I would not generally recommend the use of this rule by Conservatives. When you are able to see this tactic in use, its weaknesses become obvious, and it is then quite easy to defeat.

# Examples

By way of example, Alinsky recounts the following story in **Rules for Radicals.**

> There is a particular department store that happens to cater to the carriage trade. It attracts many customers on the basis of its labels as well as the quality of its merchandise. Because of this, economic boycotts had failed to deter even the black middle class from shopping there. At the time its employment policies were more restrictive than those of the other stores. Blacks were hired for only the most menial jobs. We made up a tactic. A busy Saturday shopping date was selected. Approximately 3,000 blacks all dressed up in their good churchgoing suits or dress would be bused downtown. When you put 3,000 blacks on the main floor of a store, even one that covers a square block, suddenly the entire color of the store changes. Any white coming through the revolving doors would take one pop-eyed look and assume that somehow he had stepped into Africa. He would keep right on going out of the store. This would end the white trade for the day.[69]

Setting aside the obvious racism in Alinsky's writing, let's consider the strategy itself. On the surface, such an approach seems formidable. After all, they are disrupting the ability of the store to make money, and they are doing nothing illegal in the process. Therefore, at first blush, it would seem difficult to counteract.

Before I discuss how to counteract such tactics let me just say that the intentions of Alinsky and those he organized were, in this case, quite laudable. After all, it is only right that a store should not discriminate and that they should hire minorities to work on the floor and in management. However, just because the goal is laudable doesn't mean the tactics are moral. This goes back to Alinsky's use of "means and ends", which we discussed in the previous chapter.

Let me offer you a few more examples of how it is used. First, in his biography of Alinsky Sanford D. Horwitt recalls certain unusual tactics undertaken by Alinsky including,

> "...dumping a mound of garbage in front of a tavern owned by the wife of an alderman, to protest his unresponsiveness to complaints of inadequate garbage pickup..."

This tactic would seem to be still on the minds of Obama's supporters. In an article by FreeRepublic.com entitled ACORN, Obama behind Plan to Dump Garbage on Speaker Boehner's Home?

> The Democratic Party is officially encouraging supporters to go to Speaker John Boehner's house and dump garbage on his lawn in order to intimidate him into rubber-stamping President Obama's destructive spending spree. Such protests can easily turn violent, especially with the tense, hyper-partisan atmosphere on Capitol Hill right now.[70]

Boycotts are typically the standard way of using this tactic. You may remember the recent use of boycotts and threats of boycotts from the State Unions in Wisconsin. This is a perfect example of how the threat is often more terrifying than the thing itself. In Wisconsin, the unions threatened to boycott businesses that did not display signs showing their solidarity with the unions.

So what is the answer to such bullying tactics? It's actually rather simple. Since Alinsky adds so little to his discussion of this particular rule, I will take a few paragraphs to explain how to counter this tactic. In the examples not involving boycotts, you simply have to remain calm. Don't allow the shock value of the tactic to make you act. Be patient and realize that the effort to perform such tactics is immense, and the threat is indeed more powerful than the thing itself. Remember that the key to all Alinsky tactics is that "the action is in the reaction". How long do you think they can get African-Americans to form large groups and pretend to shop all day? How many times do you think you can get away with throwing garbage on the sidewalk before you're fined and/or arrested? Time is on your side. The effort to perform such tactics is just too intensive and expensive, and the odds of waiting them out are very much in your favor. If you allow them to goad you and guide you in your reaction, you have already lost.

One of the main points of Alinsky tactics is to pressure you into reacting before you have a chance to think things through. If they are doing the acting, and you're doing the reacting – they are in control. The action is in the reaction.

On the other hand, how do you deal with boycotts? First, realize that the vast majority of boycotts fail. Again, time is on your side. Be watchful and patient. An alternative for boycotts like the one in Wisconsin would be to put up the sign the Unions demanded, but with a post next to it or on it that said, "This sign placed her by the local Unions." By adding such a message, you inform customers that you are cooperating against your will; this only demonstrates the bully tactics being used. The potential for a backlash by the people against the Unions is great. Such a tactic would require the Unions to become even more forceful and possibly, illegally, to force you to remove your own sign or they would have to back away. Meanwhile, everyone who saw the sign would not only know you're not supporting the Unions, but know that the Unions are using strong-arm tactics. In the end, it is always about forcing your opponent to react. When people are reacting instead of acting, they are much more likely to make mistakes, and this plays right into your hand.

## Summary

Often, things can be made to look much more threatening than they really are. This is reminiscent of rule one, "Power is not only what you have, but what people think you have". Threats of boycotts and marches are frequently intimidating – especially to small businesses. Stay calm, don't overreact, and think of creative ways to both expose those doing the threatening, and put pressure on them to act illegally.

## Rule 10 - The major premise for tactics is the development of operations that will maintain a constant pressure upon the opposition.

## Explanation

Rule ten says,

> The tenth rule: The major premise for tactics is the development of operations that will maintain a constant pressure upon the opposition. This unceasing pressure results in the reactions from the opposition that are essential for the success of the campaign. It should be remembered not only that the action is in the reaction but that action is itself the consequence of reaction and of reaction to the reaction, ad infinitum. The pressure produces the reaction, and constant pressure sustains action.[71]

The tenth rule describes what I like to refer to as *The Alinsky Reaction Chain*. The Alinsky Reaction Chain is just my way of describing what Alinsky says in his description of the tenth rule. Namely, that each action is the result of a reaction to a previous action. This cycle is continuous.

Either you control this chain of reactions, or it is controlling you. The object is to set some action into motion. This action then causes your opponent to react. Usually, reactions are emotional and lead to additional areas that can be exploited. A person skilled in Alinsky tactics can take you from calm and unsuspecting to completely out of control by simply controlling this reaction chain.

Of the thirteen rules listed by Alinsky, the two that are most likely to be recognized and understood by the majority of those even casually familiar with the Alinsky model are rule five (ridicule) and thirteen (targeting, freezing, and polarizing). However, the essence of what makes the Alinsky model so successful, and adaptable is actually rule ten. It's all about the pressure.

## Examples

The Grand Canyon is truly one of the great wonders of the world. It is staggering to think that a hole some 277 miles long, up to eighteen miles wide, and as much as a mile deep in places was carved through the solid stone by the steady and inexorable pressure of the Colorado River over the course of millions of years. The power analogized by this type of pressure was not lost on Alinsky. Stronger pressure is more efficacious, but even seemingly inconsequential pressure can produce mind-boggling results when it is applied consistently and over a sufficient length of time. Herein lays the secret not only to Alinsky's tenth rule, but also to the deceptively simple power of the Alinsky model taken as a whole.

A famous picture shows a straw embedded into the trunk of a tree. Now, straw clearly doesn't seem capable of penetrating the trunk of a tree, but the strength to perform this seemingly miraculous feat lays not in the straw itself but in the pressure applied to the straw by the wind - in this case, a tornado. This is the key to the tenth rule. The Alinsky model is designed to transfer power to the powerless, and the primary method by which it succeeds in doing this is through the same disposition of an ostensibly powerless element caught in the grip of an implacable force sufficient to apply the necessary pressure to do what might otherwise seem impossible.

As mentioned above, it took constant and varied pressure by the Obama Administration to get his signature piece of legislation passed. The Affordable Care Act – or Obamacare – was not an easy sell, but Obama and his team refused to take no for an answer. They brought various types and degrees of pressure to bear, and were ultimately able push the legislation through. Like the Colorado River, it is this ability to adapt but complete refusal to be stopped that creates the most dramatic results.

A perfect example of, "... the development of operations that will maintain a constant pressure upon the opposition..." is Obama's transformation of *Obama for America* into *Organizing for America*. According to NewsMax.com,

> "As president, I will need the help of all Americans to meet the challenges that lie ahead. That's why I'm asking people like you who fought for change during the campaign to keep fighting for change in your communities," Obama said in a Jan. 15 Internet address announcing the establishment of Organizing for America.
>
> Obama told his supporters their mass support would be essential to keeping the pressure on Washington to accomplish his goals.[72]

Notice that President Obama shows his mastery of Alinsky by dovetailing the comment about "keeping the pressure on" with his development of operations to maintain that pressure. Clearly, Obama is thinking and speaking in the context of Alinsky's tenth rule. The importance of understanding this rule cannot be overstated. Alinsky himself refers to it as "the major premise". Rule ten is the central concept of the Alinsky model. Everything the community organizer does should be done as a way to develop constant and varied pressure on the enemy. This pressure is essential to force reactions from the opponent that, in turn, can be used to increase the pressure until the Have-nots bring down the Haves.

## Summary

Pressure is the key to the Alinsky model. It needs to varied and unstoppable, like the Colorado River carving out the Grand Canyon. Pressure provokes mistakes. Mistakes allow for additional pressure. This is *The Alinsky Reaction Chain* and it is the key to successfully implementing Alinsky tactics.

## Rule 11 - If you push a negative hard and deep enough it will break through into its counterside.

# Explanation

The eleventh rule is:

> If you push a negative hard and deep enough it will break through into its counterside.; this is based on the principle that every positive has its negative.[53]

Be honest. Do you even really know what that means in terms of Alinsky tactics? It is not immediately obvious. In *Rules for Radicals,* Alinsky follows up his statement of the eleventh rule by saying,

> "We have already seen the conversion of the negative into the positive, in Mahatma Gandhi's development of the tactic of passive resistance."[53]

In addition, he follows that with a story, and it is in that story that the true meaning of the eleventh rule becomes evident. Let me first address the Gandhi reference and if you will permit me to quote the story that follows at some length perhaps, I can shed some light on this rather enigmatic Alinsky principle.

First, how does Gandhi illustrate the idea of pushing a negative through to its counter side? Gandhi, and later Dr. Martin Luther King Jr., discovered the power of the negative to accomplish positive results. When faced with clear inequities it is common to choose some display of force as the remedy. It is human nature to push back when pushed. The revolutionary methodology of Gandhi was to resist force not with force, but with passivity. In addition, as with Martin Luther King Jr., a new method of revolution was discovered and implemented. By using a negative, they were able to bring about profoundly positive change. While the concept was not new, dating back to the teaching of Jesus and others, it was a fresh execution of these tactics in a vastly different world.

Now for the story Alinsky recites after the eleventh rule in *Rules for Radicals*,

> "One corporation we organized against responded to the continuous application of pressure by burglarizing my home, and then using the keys taken in the burglary to burglarize the offices of the Industrial Areas Foundation where I work. The panic in this corporation was clear from the nature of the burglaries, for nothing was taken in either burglary to make it seem that the thieves were interested in ordinary loot – they took only the records that applied to the corporation. Even the most amateurish burglar would have had more sense than to do what the private detective agency hired by that corporation did. The police departments in California and Chicago agreed, "The Corporation might just as well have left its fingerprints all over the place."[53]

Alinsky says further,

"When a corporation bungles like the one that burglarized my home and office, my visible public reaction is shock, horror, and moral outrage. In this case, we let it be known that eventually it would be confronted with this crime as well as with a whole series of other derelictions, before a United States Senate Sub-committee Investigation. Once sworn in, with congressional immunity, we would make this action public. This threat, plus the fact that an attempt on my life has been made in Southern California, had the corporation on a spot where it would be publicly suspect in the event of assassination."[53]

Finally, Alinsky concluded,

"At one point I found myself in a thirty-room motel in which every other room was occupied by their security men. This became another devil in the closet to haunt this corporation and to keep the pressure on."[53]

Here again, we see an example of how the negative can actually be transformed into a positive when it is handled skillfully. By shining the light on the negative actions of the corporation, and making it clear, that those actions could and would become known in an unflattering manner Alinsky was able to turn the situation around to his benefit. This is not unlike the fourth rule – make the enemy live up to his own book of rules. It is by causing your opponent to act in a way that is inconsistent with his own stated rules that you gain the upper hand.

Another critical element of the eleventh rule is time. It takes time to win a battle of attrition like this. For Gandhi or Martin Luther King Jr., I'm certain that there was no belief on their part that they could make such profound changes in society overnight. Even so, Alinsky says,

> "The pressure of time should be ever-present in the mind of the tactician as he begins to engage in action."[73]

While this is true for every tactic, it is even truer for the eleventh rule, which hinges upon taking the high ground, and holding it until the other side relents.

Notice also that Alinsky's conclusion was that it was successful because it allowed him to keep the pressure on. Never lose sight of the fact that the entire emphasis of the Alinsky model is to keep the pressure on at all times. He who maintains the pressure eventually wins the battle.

## Examples

For a more modern and relevant example of how the eleventh rule is still being used we need look no further than the constant use of class warfare by the Obama Administration. To the Obama Administration it is the so-called "fat cats" on Wall Street with more money than they know what to do with that are creating the suffering for the "have-nots" in society. It is no wonder that Obama and the Left have such a soft spot in their hearts for the likes of Occupy Wall Street (OWS). Leaving aside the Marxist overtones, and the fact that Obama engages in crony capitalism with the so-called "fat cats" he maligns, let us examine how this class warfare strategy is merely an extension of the eleventh rule.

Keep pushing that negative. Keep the pressure on. Keep reminding the public of the disparity of income at every turn. Never mind the fact that the income disparity in America is far less than in other countries, or that even the poorest Americans are rich by world standards, or the fact that the poorest Americans are trapped in poverty by the very entitlement programs that President Obama espouses. Putting all that aside, we can see that the strategy is to remind poor people that they are poor, and to blame their poverty on the rich. Keep pitting the 99% against the 1%, and disregard that fact that everyone in the 99% wants the opportunity to become one of those in the 1%.

However, if you are poor, are you poor because someone else is rich? Well, possibly if that person stole the money they now possess from you, but otherwise not so much. Wealth is not a zero sum game, but class warfare is an effective tool for inciting discontent amongst both groups. The poor are irate that they have to watch the lavish lifestyles of the rich without participating, while the rich are incited by the same strategy, as they fear that the Government will seek to take their wealth and redistribute it.

Again, putting aside the clear Marxism here let us consider how this is just another way in which the Obama Administration continues to live its political life by *Rules for Radicals*. Remember that the eleventh rule seeks to push a negative hard and deep enough so that it will break through to its counterside, and that the fundamental principle of all of Alinsky's teaching is that change comes to those who maintain the proper pressure. Class warfare fits the bill perfectly.

By pushing the negative of income disparity, the Administration is able to plead their case to the American public in a way that makes the Republicans sound like heartless "super-capitalists" who would rather let the poor starve than allow any wealthy American to see a dime in tax increases. By forward-loading spending cuts into future years that are not binding on future Congresses, and by accepting millions in donations from the very wealthy Americans Obama excoriates, he is also able to apply pressure both on Congress and Wall Street in such a way that they appear to be the ones responsible for America's economic woes.

Meanwhile, joblessness and crony capitalism thrive while absolutely nothing Obama is doing is helping to ameliorate either problem, but fixing the problem is not the goal. Fixing things is never the goal of Alinsky tactics. Alinsky tactics are always designed to agitate, not mitigate. The use of Alinsky's rule 11 redounds not to the greater good of Americans rich or poor, but rather to the political fortunes of one man – Barack Obama.

OWS is just a way for the Left to attempt to imitate Gandhi or Martin Luther King Jr. The idea is to have the poor juxtaposed with the rich by placing them on Wall Street. Surely, all of America would see the inequity, and side with OWS. Unfortunately, for OWS and the Left, they were unable to behave themselves. Their rowdy and filthy behavior was bad enough, but when OWS turned violent in different cities across the nation, the support of average Americans was lost. Imagine if Martin Luther King Jr. had encouraged African-Americans to become violent. You can only push a negative through to a positive if you show the other side is acting wrongly. Once you become as bad or worse than the people whose behavior you are trying to highlight, you have lost the war.

## Summary

Harkening back to his moral dualism, Alinsky tells us now that a negative can be pushed hard enough that it becomes a positive. In other words, if you can expose an inequity in society long enough, and loudly enough, you can turn the negative you are spotlighting into positive change.

## *Rule 12 - The price of a successful attack is a constructive alternative.*

## Explanation

> The twelfth rule: The price of a successful attack is a constructive alternative. You cannot risk being trapped by the enemy in his sudden agreement with your demand and saying, "You're right – we don't know what to do about this issue. Now you tell us.[74]

We will see more of this thought in rule thirteen, when we discuss targeting the enemy. One of the ways in which a "target" can wriggle off the hook is essentially to throw his hands up in the air and say, "You're right. Now, what should we do about it?" While this is not always an effective means of refuting Alinsky tactics, it can be.

In fact, it is in his explanation of rule thirteen that Alinsky cites the following story, but I will use it here to illustrate how the twelfth rule is such an apt warning for those who would employ Alinsky tactics. Alinsky is discussing a situation where he was trying to bring integration into public schools. He says that they chose to target (this term is explained in rule thirteen) the school superintendent to be the face of the segregation problem in that area of Chicago. Alinsky says,

> "They took the position that they did not even have any racial-identification data in their files, so they did not know which of their students were black and which were white. As for the fact that we had all-white schools and all-black schools, well, that's just the way it was.

> If we had been confronted with a politically sophisticated school superintendent he could have very well replied, "Look, when I came to Chicago the city school system was following, as it is now, a neighborhood school policy. Chicago's neighborhoods are segregated. There are white neighborhoods and black neighborhoods and therefore you have white schools and black schools. Why attack me? Why not attack the segregated neighborhoods and change them?" He would have had a valid point, of sorts; I still shiver when I think of this possibility..."[75]

While the response that Alinsky describes does illustrate how the superintendent could have removed the target from his own chest, it also illustrates the twelfth rule. The superintendent would have been essentially saying, "It's not my fault. Yes, you have the wrong guy, but you've also got the wrong goal, and what's worse, you don't have a solution." It is no wonder that a response like that would have Alinsky shaking all those years later. He knew that by not fully understanding what to do with a reaction from his opponent, he was setting himself up to have the tables turned on him. The older Alinsky could see the risk, which the younger Alinsky had not seen. In using the tactics, you must be like an attorney. Attorneys are instructed never to ask a question of a witness unless you already know the answer.

With rule twelve, Alinsky is instructing community organizers to make sure that they can still maintain the pressure, and the upper hand regardless of how the enemy responds to the tactic. Never leave yourself in the position to be grandstanded by someone simply throwing up his or her hands and saying, if you're so smart, you tell us the solution.

# Examples

Why do you think the Obama Administration had to keep calling the GOP "The Party of No"? Why did they seem oblivious to the ideas that the Republican Party put forth on health care? The reason is simple – they couldn't afford to have the other side coming forward with a constructive solution while they were claiming that the system was so broken that their overhaul was the only way to fix it. They knew that Obamacare was an overreach, and to protect themselves from having the tables turned on them, they had to paint the other side as being devoid of any solution in the matter. Had they not, the ideas put forth by the GOP would have put the Left in the situation of having to go with which ever idea was more popular, rather than the ideologically driven idea they were proposing.

It would never have done simply to ask the Republicans first what solutions they had to offer, and then actually listen to them. While this may well have been the best thing for the country, it would certainly not have been the best strategic move they could make to push their agenda. You'll recall that the Democrats had an overwhelming majority in the House and even a filibuster-proof majority in the Senate for quite awhile. Their real problem was not Republicans it was Democrats. They couldn't get their own Party to agree, and so they could not leave themselves open to a "constructive alternative". Instead, they had to preempt such an attack by labeling the Republican Party as the Party of no.

## *Summary*

"The price of a successful attack is a constructive alternative". The community organizer must consider the risk that, even though he may have successfully targeted an enemy, he might leave himself open to his opponent conceding that there is a problem, and he does not know the answer. He can then simply throw up his hands and demand that you solve the problem.

## *Rule 13 - Pick the target, freeze it, personalize it, and polarize it.*

# Explanation

Perhaps no rule so clearly defines the Obama strategy as rule thirteen. It says,

> The thirteenth rule: Pick the target, freeze it, personalize it, and polarize it.[76]

Defining Terms

Targeting: Targeting, as it is used by Alinsky in the context of this rule, means the act of selecting a person who can be used to represent a larger group. Recall that in the example cited above, Alinsky targets a school superintendent to represent the school system in the matter of school integration.

Freezing: Freezing, as it is used by Alinsky in the context of this rule, means keeping a person frozen in place as the representative of the group you are attacking. Once a person is selected as the target, you do not want to let them have a legitimate reason for pushing the blame on others. They must be frozen in place as the representative of the group being attacked.

Polarizing: Polarizing, as it is used by Alinsky in the context of this rule, means to turn the most people against the target as possible. Once you have picked a target, you freeze them in place so they can't escape, and then put pressure on to throw as much mud as possible at the target.

Alinsky explains polarizing in *Rules for Radicals*,

> The classic statement of polarization comes from Christ: "He that is not with me is against me" (Luke 11:23). He allowed no middle ground to the money-changers in the Temple. One acts decisively only in the conviction that all the angels are on one side and all the devils on the other.[77]

## Explaining the Rule

Alinsky says,

> In conflict tactics there are certain rules that the organizer should always regard as universalities. One is that the opposition must be singled out as the target and "frozen." By this, I mean that in a complex, interrelated, urban society, it becomes increasingly difficult to single out who is to blame for any particular evil.[59]

Simply put, it is much easier to attack an organization or an idea if you can 'put a face on it'. If you can find a single individual who both represents your opponent, and who, given the right spin, can be portrayed as the face of evil, you can use this person as a proxy for attacks on your adversary.

Recall the discussion about racial segregation, and the way Alinsky targeted the school superintendent. You'll recall that the Chicago schools were racially segregated, and Alinsky was attempting to bring about racial integration in the school system. Alinsky speaks of how he shuddered at the thought of facing a more sophisticated opponent in the school system effort. He muses that it would have been a simple matter for the superintendent to claim that it was not his fault. After all, his schools were only representative of the neighborhoods they served. Alinsky confesses that such a response would not only have been much more difficult to orchestrate, but that the superintendent's argument would have actually not been without some merit.

While discussing the possibility that the superintendent could have argued that it was unfair to target him, and not the policies that allowed for all-white neighborhoods in the first place Alinsky laments,

I still shiver when I think of this possibility...

Had the superintendent had that level of confrontational sophistication, Alinsky and his supporters would have been stuck attacking a group of people passing blame, in Alinsky's terms, in "a dog-chasing-his-tail pattern." He repines that such a reaction would have led him into a protracted battle, a battle that he was not equipped to undertake. The reality however is that the superintendent did not confront Alinsky in this way. Instead, he allowed himself to be targeted and frozen as the face of the injustices of the segregation in the Chicago Public School System. As a result, Alinsky was able to demonize this man unjustly in order to accomplish his goal of integration.

We must be careful to avoid confusion here. As is often the case with the Left today, Alinsky's goals were laudable. However, his methods would leave anyone with a moral center chilled rather than frozen.

# Examples

Do you remember the tactics employed shortly after Barack Obama first took office in 2009? Do you recall whom he targeted and froze as the leader of the Republican Party? The answer, as bizarre as it is true, is Rush Limbaugh. Yes, they claimed a radio personality with no tangible power in the Republican Party, and who held no public office was the head of the Republican Party. Limbaugh did possess certain other attributes that made him an appealing figure to target and freeze. He is viewed negatively by a majority of Americans, and he is a man who speaks in hyperbole, and embraces controversy.

Thus, the strategy evolved to use Limbaugh as a sort of litmus test for every politician claiming to be a Conservative. Each was forced to decide publicly if they agreed or disagreed with anything controversial that Limbaugh said. If they agreed, they were labeled as extremists. If they disagreed with Limbaugh, they were labeled as being too spineless to stand up for what the really believe, and if possible they were forced to answer personally to Limbaugh for every dissimilarity. This was an effective strategy because Limbaugh has such a large megaphone with his radio show.

Such a strategy would have been deemed too ridiculous to believe in a work of fiction, but this Alinsky tactic actually gained some traction with the American people who were not inclined to believe that their President would stoop to such tactics. America is still learning the hard lesson that this administration will use any Alinsky tactic necessary, and not think twice about the moral consequences of these methods, or whether such methods befit the office of President of the United States of America.

Another example of rule thirteen is Obama's continuous blaming of George W. Bush for everything under the sun. George W. Bush was still being blamed in the 2010 mid-term elections, and I would not be surprised to hear him blamed in the 2012 election. Expect Obama to blame Bush either by name or, more likely, to blame him by implication. Lines such as, "We inherited an economy in much worse shape than we thought", and "We have rebuilt America's name overseas", make handy ways of presenting Obama as America's savior while still blaming Bush.

In 2007 – 2008 Barack Obama made his campaign about Bush. He consistently attacked George W. Bush on the campaign trail, and not John McCain. He successfully merged the two in the minds of many Americans, and claimed that a vote for McCain was just four more years for Bush. "Change We Can Believe In" was just code for the idea that you had to vote against George W. Bush's

Party. To do otherwise would be to expect change by doing the same thing.

There is a sort of reverse side to rule thirteen. It is the idea of taking a failed policy and marrying an individual to it. Perhaps it's not so much a reverse side of rule thirteen, as much as a past tense of it. You can certainly expect that Obama's team will be ready to use this against Mitt Romney if he is the GOP nominee, and if the Supreme Court strikes down The Affordable Care Act. As absurd as it sounds, don't be surprised if you hear Obama claiming that it is Romney who is at fault for the failure of his health care bill. This past tense version of rule thirteen is a powerful way to marry a failed cause, and the person you want to attack.

## Summary

Targeting, freezing, and polarizing have made its way into the lexicon of American politics. The tactic involves finding a person to be the face of the policy you are opposing, marrying him or her to the policy, and then using every method possible to attack them personally as well as the policy.

## *Chapter Summary*

Alinsky's thirteen rules are a powerful compilation of general principles that can be used to further the community organizer's call for change. Remember, that the rules are not intended as hard and fast policies to be adopted to match the circumstances, but rather as general principles to guide you as you attempt to engage creatively the enemy. The circumstances faced in a given situation are never identical. It is absurd to think that you can take a tactic that worked before and use it again in the same way. Each situation has its own set of built in variables, which must be addressed through creative use of these guiding principles.

While the way in which the rules will be applied varies over time, the principles remain the same. If you understand these rules well, you will be well equipped to recognize their use in the future. In many cases, recognizing the rules is sufficient defense in and of itself. It allows you to be calm and react only in way that benefits you or your cause. Countering the rules, however, takes both a full knowledge of the rules, and the ability to react in creative ways. Sometimes this involves defending against them, and sometimes it requires that you go on the offensive.

In next chapter, I offer you a set of principle that can be applied in the same manner to oppose and defeat Alinsky tactics. These principles, like the Alinsky tactics, are generalized. You must be creative enough to apply them to the given set of circumstances. To know the Alinsky tactics is to know your enemy. To know the principles to defeat the Alinsky tactics is to know yourself. When you can do both, you are equipped to win the war against Alinsky tactics.

# 4

# PRINCIPLES FOR DEFEATING THE ALINSKY TACTICS

*"The supreme art of war is to subdue the enemy without fighting." — Sun Tzu, The Art of War*

## *Defeating the Alinsky Tactics*

In Rules for Radicals, Alinsky presented not a rigid set of rules to be applied in the same fashion regardless of the circumstances. He knew that the exact same set of circumstances never repeat themselves. What was needed for radicals were general guidelines that could be applied creatively to ever changing circumstances. What I present here follows in the same vein. For too long,

Conservatives have stood by meekly and allowed their opposition to use the dirtiest, most underhanded tactics to destroy them both personally and professionally. While the Alinsky tactics rely on the fact that the radicals that employ them must be willing to relinquish any claim to the higher moral ground, the principles I present here to fight those rules do not require Conservatives to forfeit their souls to save the country.

We must not concede that good must stoop to the level of evil to be victorious. I do not believe that God must become like Satan to defeat him. I cannot abide the conviction that we must relinquish our morals to defeat tactics grounded in the lack thereof. Therefore, I am presenting a set of tactics that I believe will allow anyone who is willing to learn, and who is capable of using these general principles in a creative manner to defeat the Alinsky tactics while keeping his or her morals intact.

Like Alinsky's tactics, the tactics I present here seem simple, and some may seem obvious to the point of being trivial, but I would only ask that you contemplate the possibility that the genius of Alinsky is in the generality, and simplicity of what he offers. He gives rough guidelines that allow people with the proper creativity to mold them into powerful weapons. With that as a backdrop, I would humbly request that you give the following principles the same level of consideration. And so, here we go – here are AlinskyDefeater's principles for defeating Alinsky tactics.

1.  *The first rule for defeating Alinsky tactics is to anticipate that the tactics will be used against you.*

To fail to anticipate is to fail. The opposition could not have telegraphed their intentions any clearer, and yet Conservatives are constantly caught in flat-footed surprise when they find themselves the targets of Alinsky tactics. They actually wrote a book detailing how they were going to attack, and yet candidate after candidate is defeated simply because they did not see the Alinsky tactics coming.

The old adage is, "Failing to prepare is preparing to fail". How true this is for Conservatives when met with Alinsky tactics. The previous chapter details the main tactics used. Learn them until they are second nature. Expect each and every one to be used against you, and BE PREPARED WITH A RESPONSE. It is not sufficient to know Alinsky tactics. You MUST be prepared with a response that does four things: (1) The response must adequately answer and/or deflect the charge; (2) The response must be sincere and honest; (3) The response must reveal the tactics they are using; (4) The response must flip the tactic and transfer the pressure from you to your opponent.

It is not enough simply to respond to their tactic(s) in a way that exposes the falseness of their claim, and exposes the nature of their dirty tricks. To be successful in defeating Alinsky principles, you must remember that the central tenet of Alinsky principles is, "The major premise for tactics is the development of operations that will maintain a constant pressure upon the opposition." You have to be creative, and not only answer the accusation, but do so in a manner that then places pressure upon your opponent.

They wrote a book about exactly how they intend to attack you. Read it. Learn it. Learn to defend against it.

2.    *The second rule and perhaps the most important rule for defeating Alinsky tactics is to define yourself positively before your opposition has the chance to define you.*

I offer you two examples to illustrate the importance of this principle. First, the way in which Ronald Reagan defined himself and his image of America. Reagan presented himself as a believer in America and the American people, but he did so with the understanding that the freedoms America afforded its people did not come without a price, and would surely be lost if not defended. He once said,

> Above all, we must realize that no arsenal, or no weapon in the arsenals of the world, is so formidable as the will and moral courage of free men and women. It is a weapon our adversaries in today's world do not have.

And,

> Freedom is never more than one generation away from extinction. We didn't pass it to our children in the bloodstream. It must be fought for, protected, and handed on for them to do the same.

He spoke of America as "a shining city on a hill", and was unashamed to speak of America as great and exceptional. He always promoted thankfulness for the sacrifices of those who protected our freedoms, honored hard work, and put his faith in the American people not the Federal Government.

These are just a few of the ways in which Reagan defined himself, thus denying his opposition the opportunity to define him. His opposition did their best to define him as a mindless movie actor who would be in over his head as President, but his sincerity and soaring rhetoric defined him to the American people in a way that simply would not allow such allegations to stick.

Now secondly, consider Sarah Palin. Don't get me wrong. I'm a fan of Sarah Palin, and I believe she speaks to Conservatives more convincingly and more powerfully than virtually anyone else in America today. The real mistake was not Sarah Palin's so much as John McCain's. McCain found himself with no ability to stir his Conservative base, and so he took a chance with a little-known Alaskan Governor. Little known – that was exactly the problem. Because so little was known about Sarah Palin by the average American, it was quite easy for Barack Obama's legion of opposition research operatives to paint her as unprepared, and out of the American mainstream. Obama's team did such a good job of defining Palin before she could define herself that the new term "Palinization" was coined. It did not matter that most of the things said about her were complete fabrications. Once the seeds of doubt had been planted in the minds of the American people, the damage was done. There was no time to repair her image before the election. In fact, to this day, many people still believe that it was Sarah Palin, and not Tina Fey portraying her on Saturday Night Live, that said she could see Russia from her house. Once the lie takes hold, the truth has no chance.

You simply cannot allow the opposition to define you! A viable candidate must have either a proven record, or a strong vibrant story that cannot be disassembled, or both. Define yourself, or they will define you, and they don't think twice about lying and fabricating whatever is needed to make you look whatever way they feel will make you easiest for them to defeat.

Either you make it crystal clear to the people exactly who you are, warts and all, and exactly what you stand for, or your rival will invent a caricature or you that you will never live down. It's your choice – define yourself, or be defined by your opposition. Define yourself positively. Americans demand a positive leader. Believe in America. Believe in Americans, and let them know it every chance you get.

3. *The third rule in defeating Alinksy tactics is to use ridicule to your advantage.*

There are two things to keep in mind when using ridicule: (1) ridiculing your opponent can be effective if it is funny and not mean-spirited; (2) ridiculing yourself in a self-deprecating manner can be just as effective as ridiculing your opponent.

Too many people who are new to the Alinsky tactics seize on his principle of ridicule, and run with it with no regard for how it changes them in the process. Ridicule can be effective, but it can also be addictive, and cause you to become the very type of person you are seeking to ridicule. Use caution!

If you can walk that thin line where you ridicule your opponent with humor and a soft touch of humanity, you can use this tactic. If, on the other hand, you ridicule people from a place of anger and bitterness, you would be well advised to avoid this tactic altogether.

Let me give you a few examples of ridicule that are either clever, funny, sympathetic, or all of the above. Forgive my hubris in citing some of my own tweets to illustrate how properly to use ridicule.

Consider this tweet of mine – "How can you tell when a Liberal is dead? Answer: They stop calling you a racist." This is ridicule, but it is done in a way that is somewhat clever, a bit humorous, and perhaps most importantly – not directed at a single individual. If you don't call people racists, you should not be insulted by such a remark. If you are too quick to paint your opponent as racist, perhaps a little humor will give you pause. If not, the tweet succeeds in humorously illustrating something that all Conservatives on twitter feel at one time or another. From the beginning, any criticism of President Obama was labeled racist. Let me hasten to add that any hint of racism is exactly the WRONG MESSAGE to send. If you examine something you want to say, and you can find any way to construe it as racist – DON'T SAY IT!

Consider another tweet – "A penny saved is a penny . . . that Barack Obama will attempt to redistribute." Why does this work? Not only does it play off of an adage with which we are all familiar, but it addresses a major concern that many Americans have with our current President, namely, that he wants to redistribute wealth. The tweet offers a touch of humor, and not hints or overtones of anything racist or personal. It's simply an attack on policies with which so many of us disagree. The bottom line is avoiding the personal and the hateful, and embracing the humorous and the meaningful. If you're not sure if the ridicule you intend to use is proper, then don't use it, or at the very least, make sure you run it by some other people first.

But there is another side to ridicule. Self deprecating ridicule can be extremely effective. I think I can illustrate this adequately with a single example. We need only recall the second debate in 1984 between incumbent President Ronald Reagan, and challenger Walter Mondale. In the first debate, Mondale had appeared sharp, and in command of the facts while Reagan had appeared halting, confused, and frankly, a bit old. In the second debate, Reagan was able to completely resurrect a spiraling reelection campaign with a single self-deprecating line. Mondale had raised the issue of Reagan's age. He was the oldest serving President at that time at the age of 73. When the moderator raised the question of Reagan's age, and whether he still had the vigor to handle the office of President of the United States, Reagan famously answered,

> "I will not make age an issue of this campaign. I am not going to exploit, for political purposes, my opponent's youth and inexperience."

The TV camera turned to Mondale, who obviously had found the remark humorous, and was laughing at the President's remark. Mondale later remarked about that incident,

> If TV can tell the truth, as you say it can, you'll see that I was smiling. But I think if you come in close, you'll see some tears coming down because I knew he had gotten me there. That was really the end of my campaign that night, I think. [I told my wife] the campaign was over, and it was.[1]

Ridicule works both ways. If you can make the other person's position seem ludicrous through humor, then by all means do so. If, on the other hand, you can direct that humor at yourself in a way that makes your point, then do that.

4. *The fourth rule for defeating Alinsky tactics is to emulate their use of Alinsky's fourth rule – make them live up to their own book of rules.*

This particular issue is one that has long driven me to distraction. Why do Conservatives sit idly by and accept that they are to be held to a higher moral standard simply because they aspire to a higher morality? If I just fail to mention anything about any moral standard to which I intend to hold myself, does that then give me license to behave in the most despicable ways conceivable and remain impervious to criticism? If, on the other hand, I tell people that I will endeavor to uphold the highest moral standards possible, and then fall short, does that make me worse than someone who never even considers the moral implications of their actions?

Obviously, painting yourself as holier-than-thou, and then finding yourself caught in an act of debauchery opens you to rightful claims of hypocrisy, but a person who commits the same debauchery, without having first made any claim to morality is still guilty of the same impropriety and should be held to the same moral standard. Conservatives should speak less of morality, and demonstrate more of it, and all the while, they should be pointing out the immorality of the opposition for which they hold themselves unaccountable. Wrong is wrong, and the person acting with impropriety should be held accountable regardless of which Party he or she happens to represent.

The big lesson here for Conservatives is to live their morals more, and speak them less. As Ralph Waldo Emerson said, "What you do speaks so loudly that I cannot hear what you say". Emerson also offered excellent advice for Conservatives when he said, "If you would lift me up you must be on higher ground."

Keeping yourself above reproach is only half of the equation. Recall that Alinsky's fourth rule says, "Make the enemy live up to their own book of rules". Liberals are frequently unrealistically idealistic. Like Barack Obama in his acceptance speech claiming that someday the world would look back and say that today was the day the seas began to recede. Take note of their claims, even if you don't agree with their intentions, and remind them constantly of how they have failed to accomplish what they promised. Remind your opponent often how their idealistic notions have been abandoned because they were simply unrealistic to begin with. Wealthy Liberals are always ready to launch into a tirade about the disparity between the rich and the poor in America. When it comes to actually giving of their massive wealth to help the poor, you will find them wanting. The same is true when they speak of the disparity in the tax code. Have they volunteered to give additional taxes to the IRS through its website? Have they eschewed available tax loopholes when filing their taxes? There are dozens of such inconsistencies by the Left, and they are seldom called on them. Research issues where Liberals are inconsistent, and hammer them with it every chance you get!

*5.    The fifth rule for defeating Alinsky tactics is to force your opponent to back up any and all accusations made against you.*

If the claim is legitimate, then take it head on. If it was a mistake, admit it and explain what you learned. However, Conservatives are notorious for allowing baseless claims to linger in the air. If your opponent accuses you of some impropriety or inconsistency, demand that they prove their accusations. If they cannot, remind them that baseless accusations can be made against anyone, and if they would prefer that such accusations not be levied against them, then they should refrain from the same. As Alinsky himself put it, "The threat is usually more terrifying than the thing itself".

As an adjunct, you can repeat their ridiculous overreaches such as claims that Romney wants to go back to a time when blacks and women couldn't vote. Having proxies repeat how ridiculous remarks like these are ad nauseum can be quite effective as long as you are absolutely certain everyone will see how ridiculous and incorrect the statements are. This last part is critical if this tactic is to be used.

6.   *The sixth rule for defeating Alinsky tactics is to refuse to be targeted, and refuse to be smeared with the deeds of others.*

This is one of the most effective traps the Alinskyites have. You have to be on the alert for it at all times, and not allow yourself to be snared by it. During the 2008 Presidential campaign Barack Obama was able to target and freeze McCain as representing "just another Bush term". It wasn't until the final debate that McCain finally told Obama, "I'm not George Bush". This came way too late and allowed Obama to define McCain for months as the second coming of George W. Bush, who had an abysmal popularity rating at the time.

It is critical that you do not let yourself become the poster boy for any unpopular or unsound policy, especially if you had nothing to do with it. This is a favorite tactic of Alinskyites, and you have to stop it immediately. Never let anyone put words from someone else in your mouth just because you share the same Party label. They want you to either accept the label or turn on someone else in your own Party and start disparaging them. Don't fall for either. Simply point out that it is not your policy, and it is not what you would do, and leave it at that.

7. *The seventh rule for defeating Alinsky tactics is to fight fire with fire.*

One of the Obama Administration's favorite tactics is to try to paint Republicans as "extremists". Every GOP plan is characterized as extreme, and far out of the main stream. They actually invited the "birther" debate just to paint people as extremists. When the "extremist" card is played against you, play one right back at them. A famous Democratic commercial had a lookalike of Paul Ryan tossing an old woman off a cliff, because Ryan proposed changes to help keep Medicare viable. Such an attack should have been met with a similar ad showing how Obamacare actually is cutting $500 Billion from Medicare, gutting Medicare gold plans, and trying to deny women mammograms. Who's the extremist?

This one should be so easy, and obvious that I won't spend a great deal of time on it. I will say, "DO IT!" Waiting around and acting as though everyone is just going to figure out how crazy their attacks are WILL NOT WORK.

8.    *The eighth rule for defeating Alinsky tactics is to embrace religion, and not run from it.*

This is not a losing issue for Conservatives, but it MUST be framed properly. The numbers are on our side, but the Left has the advantage of fractionalizing the religious communities, and painting all people of religion as anti-science and fanatical. I'm not saying this is true, I'm saying the Left is framing it that way, and the Right is failing to make an effective argument against it.

Frame religion in the context of the faith of the founding Fathers, and point out the millions of God-fearing Americans of every faith who make America a better place to raise our children every day. Remind your opponent that the first Amendment is one of the most transformative, and liberating laws in human history.

The religious issue can also be played in a negative way. This is not the optimal choice, but when presented with the kind of ammunition that the Jeremiah Wright controversy afforded the GOP in 2008, it was a ridiculously poor choice to avoid using it in the general election. A simple ad with Jeremiah Wright declaring, "God damn America", with the question, "Can you honestly believe that Barack Obama listened to this man for 20 years, and didn't know he had anti-American views?" would have been remarkably effective.

9. *The ninth rule for defeating Alinsky tactics is to use what your opposition gives you.*

Don't miss a fastball down the middle of the plate. Every politician makes mistakes, and you have to be ready to pounce. Also, do EXTREME opposition research. The Left has made some outrageous claims, and backed some ridiculous plans – don't let them off the hook. Conservatives are usually pretty good at this one, but it is still important. Energy from algae, misleading statements about domestic oil production, tax promises, Solyndra, and Obama's claims that he embraces an "all of the above" energy policy now when he ran against it in 2008, are just some of the issues that Conservatives can hammer the Left on. Certainly there will be plenty more mistakes made before the 2012 election takes place, and Conservatives need to be ready, and not miss a chance to hammer the Left on mistakes when they are made.

10. *The tenth rule for defeating Alinsky tactics is to take away their talking points.*

They aren't hard to find. They repeat them ad nauseum. If a claim is not true, prove it false. If it is true, admit it. The important thing is to not let it fester. Make them change talking points constantly. They're not creative enough to come up with new talking points repeatedly.

11.    *The eleventh rule to defeating Alinsky tactics is to be open and honest about your faults and failures from the outset.*

Be open and honest. Never hide a fault. The cover-up is almost always worse than the offense. It is much better to be honest about any mistakes you've made than to try to spin them. If your position on an issue has evolved, then admit it and explain what changed your mind. Remember, even Ronald Reagan was a Democrat at one time.

12.    *The twelfth rule to defeating Alinsky tactics is – never apologize for success, and extol the virtues of opportunity and individual achievement.*

Americans respect success. Americans believe in the opportunity for success more than they do in entitlement. Apologizing for success is like apologizing for the American dream. Don't run from success, seek only to assure that the playing field will be fair, and appeal to the desire in every American to improve his lot in life, and to provide a better life for his or her children, and grandchildren. At the same time, don't forget that there are those in our society that need a safety net. The important thing is to remember that the key word in that sentence is "need".

13.    *The thirteenth rule for defeating Alinsky tactics is always to make your argument, and your candidacy, about America.*

Americans love their country. You can't believe in it enough. They want to know you believe in America, and you believe in their ability to make America better. You can preach that American decline has occurred under your opponents Administration, but you MUST follow that with how you will restore America, and how through the ingenuity of the American people, America's best days are still square in front of her. NEVER apologize for America!

*14. The fourteenth rule to defeating Alinsky tactics is not to allow yourself to be lumped in with any group or any less than flattering ideology.*

Never accept a label that makes you appear weak or extreme. Point out stark contrasts between who you are, and what you believe as opposed to the allegations against you. You are not required to approve or disapprove of every idea or thought presented by every Conservative in the country. You don't have to answer for what Rush Limbaugh or some member of Congress says. State your position, and assert the other person's right to speak their mind, and offer their opinions.

*15. The fifteenth rule to defeating Alinsky tactics is always to project America as strong.*

Americans may believe America is in decline in the world, but they don't want to hear their leaders admit it. Instead, they want their leaders to project the confidence that they can lead America back to its rightful place of prominence in the world. Make your position a clear and stark contrast with those who choose to blame America first, and who choose to criticize everything America does without offering solutions or extolling her virtues. There is nothing wrong with admitting America is not perfect, but always appeal to the higher aspirations and more noble nature of Americans.

16. *The sixteenth rule for defeating the Alinsky tactics is to think more than one move ahead.*

Politics is a game of chess, not checkers. Alinsky's entire premise was the continual use of pressure to cause reactions. You MUST think several moves ahead. How will what you propose be met, and how will you respond? How will your response be responded to, and how will you answer, etc.? Alinsky put it this way,

> It should be remembered not only that the action is in the reaction but that action is itself the consequence of reaction and of reaction to the reaction, ad infinitum. The pressure produces the reaction, and constant pressure sustains action.[2]

This rule cannot be overemphasized, because it is the central premise of all of Alinsky's tactics. Lazy thinking and the failure to anticipate what your opponent may do is a certain prescription for failure.

17.   *The seventeenth rule for defeating the Alinksy tactics is to know both sides of the issue.*

It should be the job of the committed Conservative to study the opposing view point thoroughly. Read books, websites and news with a Liberal slant. Know not only what their positions are, but why they hold them. This type of intellectual honesty will only reinforce your own convictions while allowing you to gain the knowledge necessary to deconstruct your opponents' point of view. You can't defeat a well-informed Liberal if you only read and listen to Conservative points of view. Know their side as well as you know yours.

18.   *The eighteenth rule for defeating Alinsky tactics is to control the pressure.*

Always force your opponent to react.

Within the Alinsky paradigm, the best defense is a good offense. It is always preferable for the Alinskyite to keep the pressure on. Logic and cohesiveness of thought are unimportant to the agitator. He or she is simply attempting to roil you, and provoke you into responding emotionally rather than thoughtfully. Remember, it is always easier to tear something down than it is to build it. Alinskyites will use whatever method that is at their disposal to throw you off your game. They are not trying to prove a point or win a logical battle. They are attempting to get you to react in a way that they can then use against you. Don't make the mistake of believing that Alinskyites are interested in serious political dialogue. They are not! They are interested in getting you to act the fool. They are interested in tearing you down, not constructive dialogue. This is why endless battles on twitter and Facebook with Liberals are fruitless endeavors. They are only designed to keep you from exposing this Administrations lies, and putting forth positive alternatives.

19. *The nineteenth rule for defeating Alinsky tactics is, "Don't fall for 'implied' attacks".*

Barack Obama, in particular is famous for leaving the target of his attacks in doubt, and then allowing the target to paint themselves into a corner by replying. An example is Barack Obama saying he was not born with a silver spoon in his mouth. He never mentioned Romney, and did not make the remark in the context of the campaign itself, but most people knew to whom he was referring. Romney responded to the attack. His response was sound in that he refused to apologize for his father's success, but he never should have responded at all. He should have simply said that he did not know who the President was referring to, but that the President is quite fond of criticizing success rather than inspiring all Americans to seek success. By responding, he admits Obama's claim that he was born with a silver spoon in his mouth, and allows the President to engage him on a subject where he is stronger with the majority of voters.

*20. The twentieth rule for defeating Alinsky tactics is to remember that the sooner you reveal anything that can be used against you – the sooner it will become old news.*

Failure to abide by this principle was a big factor in John McCain's loss to Barack Obama. He needed the excitement that Sarah Palin brought to the campaign, but to get it he had to introduce a mostly unknown politician to a national campaign with very little time left for any negatives about her to be revealed and discussed. It is the new stuff that gets you. A politician can have negatives, but once they have been known for awhile, they become old news. The sooner you can get a negative into the public awareness the better.

## *Chapter Summary*

I have provided twenty principles to defeat Alinsky tactics. Don't be deceived by their simplicity. Some are obvious, and some are not, but when they are used in combination and with creativity they provide a powerful way to defeat Alinsky tactics without succumbing to moral contradictions. It is critical that Conservatives do not simply adopt the Alinsky tactics. To do this would be to become the people you are claiming are amoral. The Bible says in Romans 12:21,

Do not be overcome by evil, but overcome evil with good.

The principles presented here are presented in a very basic way intentionally. The idea is not to use them like a cookbook, but rather to use each principle as a starting point for your own creative process. The same set of circumstances will never come together exactly the same way twice. You must know how to take these general principles, and adapt them creatively to whatever circumstances you encounter.

You cannot successfully defend against Alinsky tactics unless you understand them, but knowledge of the tactics alone is not enough to defeat them. To defeat them you must have a positive plan with clearly delineated methodology. Adapting the same amoral, ends justify the means tactics may be effective, but you are no longer defeating the tactics – you are just using them. Defeating the tactics means overcoming their effectiveness without falling prey to the moral equivalence upon which they rest. For any person who believes in absolute morality, the ends do not justify the means.

With the simple principles posited here you can overcome Alinsky tactics. The only limits to your effectiveness in doing so will be your understanding of the Alinsky tactics, your understanding of the principles used to defeat them, and the level of creativity you can demonstrate in applying those principles.

# 5

# *The Road Ahead*

*Can you imagine what I would do if I could do all I can? ~Sun Tzu, The Art of War*

The 2012 Presidential election promises to be one of the dirtiest Presidential Campaigns in modern American political history. Even the thin veil of civility is likely to come off as Obama squares off against Romney in the general election. Both men have already demonstrated a propensity for hitting hard with the negative ads, and pulling no punches in general. This President has shown that he is willing to a little further down in the dirt than most incumbents. His recent ad showing Bill Clinton praising him for his decision to kill Bin Laden, also asks the question of whether or not Romney would have made that decision. While it is hard to conceive of any President who would not have made that decision, Obama deserves credit for getting the job done. However, he now sabotages and taints any credit he got for getting Bin

Laden by making our national security a political football for his innuendo campaign against Romney.

Obama is left with no way to claim that Americans are better off now than they were four years ago. The two signature pieces of legislation of this Administration are problematic. First, a stimulus act that cost American taxpayers nearly a trillion dollars has been largely viewed as a complete failure. Secondly, The Affordable Care Act (a.k.a. Obamacare) is in danger of being struck down as unconstitutional by the Supreme Court before the election season hits high gear. With the American economy growing at an anemic pace, Obama's signature pieces of legislation in serious trouble, foreign affairs appearing more chaotic, and domestic gas prices at record levels, the President is not able to run on his record. The only alternative is to paint his adversary as a worse choice. Bring on the Alinsky tactics!

There are other Alinsky tactics that have been used through the years that I did not include in the chapter on Alinsky tactics. In this chapter, I will explain a few of those tactics, and offer a few predictions about what President Obama may attempt to do during this campaign. One of the nice things about understanding Alinsky tactics is that it makes it possible to anticipate some of the moves this Administration is likely to take. At the very least, it makes easy to interpret why they do certain things the way they do.

## *Other Alinsky Tactics*

***Class warfare*** is actually less a tactic than it is an underlying principle of Alinskyites, but it bears mentioning here since it is the central thesis of Alinsky's book. Class warfare is a concept borrowed from Marxism. President Obama has already given ample evidence that class warfare will be front and center in the 2012 campaign. From comments about the 1%, people not "paying their fair share", and not putting America's recovery on the backs of the poor and the middle class to his comment about not being born with a silver spoon in his mouth, Obama has shown a strong predilection to engage in class warfare; this in stark contrast with his previous statements about wanting to unite a divided country. In his convention speech for John Kerry in 2006 Obama said,

> There's not a black America and white America and Latino America and Asian America; there's the United States of America.
>
> The pundits, the pundits like to slice and dice our country into red states and blue States: red states for Republicans, blue States for Democrats. But I've got news for them, too. We worship an awesome God in the blue states, and we don't like federal agents poking around our libraries in the red states.
>
> We coach little league in the blue states and, yes, we've got some gay friends in the red states.[1]

This message seems incongruous with the man holding the office today. Much like George W. Bush who had run as a "uniter not a divider", Barack Obama has gone from the lofty rhetoric of his nomination speech to his current war on success and the successful in the United States. The same man who lauded America as a land his parents had seen where anything is possible is now telling us that people who simply pay the taxes the law says they should pay are somehow unpatriotic. It used to be the cry of the Left that people could oppose the war in Iraq and still be patriotic. Now, their message seems to be, as Joe Biden famously put it, that paying higher taxes is "the patriotic thing to do".[2]

Plants are not a new tactic, but they seem to have caught a lot of people by surprise in 2008 and 2009. Watch for this tactic in the 2012 Presidential campaign.

**Infiltration** is another tactic used by Alinsky and his followers. In fact in his biography,

When an Oregon school teacher put up a website on CrashTheTeaParty.org (the site no longer exists) it was a way of showing his fellow enthusiasts on the Left how to infiltrate Tea Party events and behave badly. The idea was to infiltrate Tea Party events dressed as Tea Partiers, but carry racist or offensive signs. The site http://zombietime.com/crashing_the_crashers/ has documentation of such attempts at a Tea Party rally in San Francisco. On at least a few other occasions, there seems to be some evidence that people were attempting to infiltrate Tea Party events, and then behave in a way that would both call attention to them and be deemed racist or offensive in some manner.[3]

**Plants** are yet another Alinsky tactic – one that President Obama has used on numerous occasions. When you read below about the "plants" that Obama used in his health care townhalls you might wonder how Obama ever dreamed he would get away with such obvious tactics. I can't say for sure, but I'm inclined to believe that the President was not used to the national spotlight at that point. He had apparently used such tactics many times before and gotten away with it so he had no reason to believe that an adoring public or a fawning media would be likely to call him out on the obvious fakes.

It would appear that the President's townhall meetings to push his health care bill were swarming with Democratic operatives. In Amnandale, Virginia one of the people to ask the President a question was a woman who said was suffering from Kidney cancer. In a heartfelt moment, the President assured her that she would get the help she needed, and he would see to it. Only a few problems with that – she didn't have cancer, and she was working as a member of Organizing for America (OFA) – Mr. Obama's political arm. This was not an isolated incident.[4]

In Portsmouth, N.H. on August 11, 2009 a little girl got up and asked the President a question about all the signs she had encountered on her way in and how many seemed to say "mean things" about the President and his health care bill. Once again there is a problem with this story. The Obama Administration continued to push the line that all the people who asked questions at the townhalls were selected at random, but that story just does not seem to be supported by the facts. Some astute reporters later revealed that the little girl with the questions about the "mean things" people were saying was an 11-year-old girl named Julia Hall. Julia's mother Kathleen was seated next to her. Kathleen Hall just happened to be a MA resident who had contributed to Barack Obama's Presidential campaign, and had met Michelle Obama and later pictures would emerge that showed Ms. Hall posing with

Barack Obama. One really has to suspend all common sense to attribute all of Barack Obama's health care plants to chance.[5]

This tactic was only a slight spin on something Alinsky had done years before. In Alinsky's case, he chose to plant members of the opposition, but the same concept is involved. In his biography of Alinsky, Sanford D. Horwitt says,

> "...in the spring of 1972, at Tulane University...students asked Alinsky to help plan a protest of a scheduled speech by George H. W. Bush, then U.S. representative to the United Nations – a speech likely to include a defense of the Nixon administration's Vietnam War policies. The students told Alinsky they were thinking about picketing or disrupting Bush's address. That's the wrong approach, he rejoined, not very creative – and besides causing a disruption might get them thrown out of school. He told them, instead, to go to hear the speech dressed as members of the Ku Klux Klan, and whenever Bush said something in defense of the Vietnam War, they should cheer and wave placards reading,

> 'The KKK supports Bush.' And that is what they did, with very successful, attention-getting results."[6]

So you can see that plants are nothing new. The truly alarming part is that Barack Obama would continue to use such dishonest and juvenile tactics as a sitting President of the United States.

***The encouragement of misconceptions*** is still another tactic employed by Alinsky and his chief disciple, Barack Obama. Alinsky used to make a point of not being pigeonholed as a communist or Marxist for the explicit purpose of appealing to as many people as possible. While his philosophy is clearly Marxist, he wanted to ensure that even people who were against Marxism and communism would support him in his causes.

Alinsky's biographer says of him,

> Alinsky had no formal affiliation with the Communist Party, but liked to think of himself as "emotionally aligned very strongly with it".[7]

So we can see that while Alinsky refused to self-identify, his philosophy was that of a Marxist. The need to 'agitate' runs to the very heart of the Marxist belief that Capitalism will end only when the people organize, and revolt against their "rich oppressors". Class warfare is at the heart of Marxism. Marxism was at the heart of Alinsky's methods, and Alinsky is at the heart of Barack Obama's methods.

Barack Obama spent much of his first term claiming he had released his birth certificate to the public. Why then did he release his long form birth certificate to the public on April 27, 2011?[8]

If he had already released his birth certificate and there supposedly was no such thing as a long form birth certificate, why wait two years into you Presidency to release the document?

I know a lot of people still believe that Obama was born in Kenya. I am not one of those people. I believe there was a much simpler reason that he didn't release the birth certificate – he was following his Alinsky training. Extremism is at the heart of the attack line of the Democratic National Committee (DNC).[9]

By allowing people to claim he was not a citizen, Obama left open the very real possibility that he could use his birth certificate to discredit them. In fact, as mentioned above, the DNC put out a mid-term strategy guide that said just that. The plan was to paint all Republicans as extremists. Of course, Obama knew that at any given moment he could pull out his birth certificate and make them look like fools. You might think I'm making this up, but after they got walloped in the 2010 mid-terms, and the only candidate crazy enough to raise the birther issue was Donald Trump, the Obama people gave up in the early spring of 2011 and just released the document.

This is a common tact on the Left. Pretend you don't believe in something or allow someone else to believe something you know you can disprove when it's convenient. I mean, do you really think that Barack Obama is against gay marriage? Do you really think he wants gas prices to come down for other than political reasons? Barack Obama is a hard core Leftist and you can bet he holds all the far-Left positions. He simply won't do things that are politically inexpedient, because he is working his Alinsky plan - get the radicals into power and change the system that way.

Working within the system is a fundamental tenet of Alinsky's teachings. In *Rules for Radicals* he says,

As an organizer I start from where the world is, as it is, not as I would like it to be…That means working in the system.

He calls himself a "radical pragmatist"[10] (R4R, p.xxi). Not unlike Alinsky, Obama is often referred to by those on the Left as "a pragmatist at heart". While most of us on the Right would disagree, the point is that he sees himself that way. Alinsky recalls his dismay at the dispatching of the National Guard to quell rioting at the 1968 Democratic National Convention,

> It hurt me to see the American army with drawn bayonets advancing on American boys and girls. But the answer I gave the young radicals seemed to me the only realistic one: "Do one of three things. One, go find a wailing wall and feel sorry for yourselves. Two, go psycho and start bombing – but this will only swing people to the right [a message that apparently never made its way to Barack Obama's friend Bill Ayers]. Three, learn a lesson. Go home, organize, build power and at the next convention, you be the delegates."

He then goes on to give would-be radicals another exhortation to action – one that Conservatives would do well to heed,

> It is not enough just to elect your candidates. You must keep the pressure on. Radicals should keep in mind Franklin D. Roosevelt's response to a reform delegation, "Okay, you've convinced me. Now go on out and bring pressure on me!" Action comes from keeping the heat on.

**Speaking in generalities** is a concept lifted straight from the pages of *Rules for Radicals*. 2008 was the "Hope and Change" election; the "Yes, we can" election. As Sarah Palin famously said, "How's that hopey changey thing workin' out for you?"

The entire book Rules for Radicals is practically littered with phrases that mirror Barack Obama's slogan of "Hope and Change". The only other concept that appears more often is also a Barack Obama slogan – change. In fact, the phrase "Change we can believe in" sounds like some sort of shortcut synopsis for *Rules for Radicals*. The theme is to accept the world as it is and change it into the world you envision. Chapter after chapter, Alinsky hammers home the ideas of hope and change. Just one example of the change centric mantra of Alinsky is,

> The organizer's job is to inseminate an invitation for himself, to agitate, introduce ideas, get people pregnant with hope and a desire for change and to identify you as the person most qualified for this purpose.11 [Emphasis added]

## *Some Predictions about the 2012*
## *Presidential Campaign*

Expect Obama to get more desperate if he is losing in October. Some ways he might react:

*Barack Obama's 2012 campaign* slogan will be simplistic and general. It is almost a certainty that Obama will continue this Alinsky tactic of over-generalizing and allowing other people to impute to it whatever interpretation is personally meaningful to them. "Hope and Change", "Change we can Believe in", and "Yes, we can" are all simplistic phrases that basically mean whatever you want them to mean. I'm not sure what golden slogan his team will cook up in 2012 but I can just about guarantee you it will be short on meaning and long on feeling.

We have already seen Barack Obama use the Presidency in ways that seem below the dignity of that august office. When he challenges whether or not Mitt Romney would have had the nerve to make the call on going after Osama Bin Laden from the White House itself, and while a foreign leader was present, it seems hard to imagine that there is anything that our current "campaigner in chief" will not politicize. Expect Obama to walk as close to the line as possible, if not over it, to further his political future. It's the kind of thing people do when they are convinced they are right, and that the end is more important than the means.

Note: The Obama Administration slightly outpaced me here. They released their new 2012 campaign slogan just two days before I put this book out. The new slogan will be – "Forward". Even I could not possibly have predicted just how mundane and nonspecific their slogan would be. You can project whatever you want onto that blank screen.

*Expect Obama to keep hammering the class warfare argument* home right up until Election Day. Unfortunately, the reason the Obama team clings to this strategy is because a majority of Americans seem to agree with him to some extent. However, I believe in the end that Obama is misreading the support he gets on this issue. While the majority of Americans tend to support some notion of the rich paying their "fair share", I don't believe that the majority of Americans have abandoned the idea of America as a land of opportunity. If you frame the question so that it appears that the so-called rich are skating by then Americans reject that. However, if you frame the question so that people are presented with either an America where equal outcomes are guaranteed or an America where equal opportunity is guaranteed, I'm reasonably sure the majority of Americans still prefer the latter. If not, we are past a tipping point in this country, and God help us.

The 2012 election will set forth two competing images of the future of our country. While many Conservatives (myself included) had hoped for a more legitimately Conservative opponent for Barack Obama, it is clear that no such viable option emerged during this election cycle. Still, Mitt Romney is a clear choice in ideology when viewed against Barack Obama. Romney sees a free market, individual responsibility, bottom-up type of Government. Obama clearly represents a top-down, fair share, collective mentality. This is one of those watershed elections that comes around once or twice in a lifetime. We were at just such a crossroads in 1980 after four years of Jimmy Carter. While Romney doesn't exactly seem like Ronald Reagan, truth be known, Reagan didn't seem like Reagan in 1980, but the country knew it couldn't tolerate four more years of Jimmy Carter. This year, I certainly hope the country realizes that it just can't afford four more years of Barack Obama. To reelect Obama is to cast a vote of confidence in his vacillating leadership, quasi-Marxist ideology, and top-down view of the Federal

Government. If the Supreme Court doesn't strike down Obamacare, it will also be a vote to confirm Obamacare and for all intents and purposes institutionalize it.

*Watch for proxy attacks by Obama in 2012*. This will be nothing new, but it may come at heretofore unseen level. Proxy attacks are attacks where the President allows someone in his Administration or perhaps someone in the Press to set forth his position or complaint about a certain issue. This allows him a level of plausible deniability about taking such a negative or extreme position.

Proxy attacks can come from just about anywhere, and they are almost always much more vicious than anything that Obama will actually say himself. As an aside here – whenever I refer to President Obama as simply Obama – I can hear the words of some Liberal demanding that I pay the President of the United States the proper respect and refer to him as President Obama. This always amuses and/or annoys me since I did not here these same people making such demands for the previous occupant of the White House. In fact, Bush is about the nicest thing I remember anybody on the Left calling President Bush, but back to the proxy attacks.

For an illustration of proxy attacks, just think back to 2008 and the Obama attacks on Sarah Palin and her family. While Barack Obama was trying to look above it all and even claimed that families were off limits, it was his operatives that took up residence in Alaska to uncover any and all dirt – real and imagined – that could be offered by the people of Alaska. Vicious rumors hounded Governor Palin, and you can be reasonably certain that those rumors began with someone, no matter how low down, on the Obama team. Frankly, the Media is so in bed with this President that some of these rumors may have come from them, but almost certainly the majority of them originated with Obama operatives. Like Alinsky himself, the Obama team revels in the chance to use any form of ridicule at its disposal, and it lives and dies with rule thirteen – target, freeze, and polarize.

A good place to watch for proxy attacks is shows like *Meet the Press*. These type of shows offer Obama underlings a chance to parade out any sort of wild idea that they want to send out as a test balloon to see how effective it might be. People like David Axelrod and David Plouffe frequent these shows, and as Election Day approaches you can expect them to have more and more explosive things to say. Another place to watch for proxy attacks is MSNBC. They basically take it upon themselves to say what Obama dare not.

*If the President is trailing in the polls, you can expect religious attacks.* This issue is an explosive one for Obama. He runs the risk of alienating a significant portion of the electorate if he is too aggressive in coming after Romney on Mormonism. At the same time, he also runs the risk that Romney can counter with the President's less than mainstream religious past. This strategy contains so much inherent risk for team Obama that you are unlikely to see it play out unless the President feels desperate. However, if the President is down in polls late, you can expect almost anything out of the Obama camp, and religious attacks are one of many possibilities.

You would think that a man who says he sat in the pews of Jeremiah Wright's church for twenty years and didn't know that he had anti-American views would not be likely to cast the first stone in a religious contest, but there are ways Obama can play this card and appear innocent. His super-PAC can certainly put forth anti-Mormon propaganda, and other proxies can do the same. Again, there is risk in this strategy so it may or may not happen depending upon where the President stands in the polls.

*You can expect Obama to play the race card if he feels the benefit will outweigh the risk*. There are a number of ways he could choose to do this, but be on the lookout for people in Obama's crowd or people in Romney's crowd that might say inflammatory things regarding race. A possible Obama tactic would be to place operatives in his own crowd who would shout out racially inflammatory comments. This would provide the President with both an opportunity to look like a victim of racism and the simultaneous opportunity to respond to the heckler in a predesigned manner. Imagine someone shouting out a racial epithet at an Obama campaign rally, and President Obama then responding in a thoughtful and unemotional manner. He could forgive the person and say that he understands that such ignorance still exist in our country but it's time to move "forward" past the days of racism in America. Such a tact would place the President in a position to appear thoughtful, rational, kind, forgiving, and somehow above the fray when it comes to matters of race.

Another possibility would be to place people in the Romney crowd to make racially insensitive remarks while appearing to be Romney supporters. This tactic is much like the one mentioned previously where Alinsky told followers to dress as KKK members and agree with George H.W. Bush during a speech. Whether it was an Obama operative or not, a similar thing happened during the 2008 campaign when an older woman got up at a

McCain rally and begin to recount her fears that Obama was dangerous and not born in America. No proof has ever been offered, to my knowledge, that this woman was an Obama operative, but it certainly would not surprise me if such proof were proffered in the future. This tactic is right in the wheelhouse of an Alinskyite.

Watch for these and other Alinsky tactics as Election Day nears. The more desperate the situation, the bolder and more blatant the tactics almost certainly will be. Do not expect this President to leave office easily or quietly. Expect a huge Alinsky-style push the longer Obama is tied or behind in the polls. The more forceful the attack, the more he risks a backlash so expect Obama to stay with the types of attacks he has used thus far if he feels he still on the path to victory, but if his Presidency seems in danger, you can expect his team to pull out all the stops and throw caution to the wind. It's going to a long, bumpy Presidential campaign and things are likely to get very strange this summer and fall; hang on, it's going to be a bumpy ride.

# *Conclusion*

In chapter one you learned a little about who Saul Alinsky was, why his work Rules for Radicals has become such an important book, and how closely aligned Barack Obama is to Alinsky. In chapter two we saw the moral bankruptcy of Alinksy tactics, and how they are just really thinly veiled Marxism. In chapter three you learned what Alinsky's thirteen main tactics are and how to recognize them;, and you also saw some examples of them in use. In chapter four you learned about my twenty principles designed to defeat the Alinsky tactics. Finally, in this chapter I have discussed a few more of Alinsky's tactics, and some things that just might take place during the present Presidential campaign.

I am not the first or the only one to discuss Alinsky and his tactics from a Conservative viewpoint. I began blogging about this subject sometime in late 2009 at http://www.AlinskyDefeater.com/Blog/ and the previous incarnation of the blog however, and many of my articles predate some of the earliest books from the Right on this subject. What I do offer in this book that is different from anything else out there is that it is not a rehashing of how Conservatives can co-op the tactics for their own use. Instead, I have offered here a rebuttal of the moral foundation of Alinsky and his tactics coupled with twenty principles you can use to defeat Alinsky tactics without sacrificing the moral high ground. In this way, this book is different than any other on the subject. It is also a practical book. I have avoided, to the level possible, the more arcane and professorial approaches to the subject in favor of a handbook that can sit beside *Rules for Radicals*, and be used to defeat it, but the book is not dumbed-down nor does it sacrifice accuracy for practicality.

Saul Alinsky is no longer a name known only to a few on the extreme Left. With the help of Barack Obama, Alinsky has become a household word for those on the Right as well. His most famous book – *Rules for Radicals* – is now studied by those wrestling for power on both sides. The thirteen most famous of Alinsky's tactics form a nucleus of Left-wing revolutionary methodology that the Right would do well to understand, but must exercise caution before attempting to use. I would encourage every Conservative to at least have a cursory knowledge of Alinsky and his tactics. If you want to contend in the political realm, or if you wish to converse about politics in places like Facebook and twitter, you would be well served by mastering the Alinsky tactics. You will doubtlessly encounter people on social media who are versed in Alinsky tactics, and are using them against you without your knowledge. Unless you understand Alinsky tactics they can be quite difficult to overcome. Most of the tactics, and the principles I put forth to combat them, are deceptively simple. Don't be fooled by this. It takes time and practice to truly understand Alinsky's tactics, and the same is true for the principles to defeat the tactics.

Barack Obama has changed the way politics is practiced at the Presidential level in this country. His use of Alinsky tactics was, at first, quite off-putting to those of us who have been around long enough to see several Presidential campaigns. Much of what he engages in seems below the dignity of the office he holds. The younger generation is not as attuned to these subtle changes. It is up to us to educate people, and share our understanding of American Exceptionalism and how the Alinsky tactics fly in the face of the moral bedrock upon which this nation is founded. I hope this book will serve as an introductory course for those who know nothing of Alinsky tactics and a guidebook for those who are engaged in politics and face the Alinsky tactics in the all-to-real world.

There is no limit to the way in which Alinsky tactics can be employed. As I mentioned before, the only limit on the application of Alinsky tactics is your creativeness in using them. When the dust finally settles on the 2012 campaign, the tactics I have explained in this book and many other Alinsky tactics will likely have been used. Hopefully, to be forewarned is to be forearmed. I hope that in some small way this book will have provided you with a keener ability to discern Alinsky tactics when they are being used, how to defend against them, and how to argue the Conservative case more effectively.

Finally, here is the bottom line for Conservative when facing Alinsky tactics. Take the high road when possible. Seek to bring out the best in your fellow man, but do not shy away from the fray when it becomes necessary to defend the traditional American values that have made this the greatest and most prosperous nation in the history of mankind. Be informed. Know the other side and the tactics they use. Practice the principles set forth in this book. Barack Obama once famously told us (perhaps warned us) that we were just days away from "fundamentally transforming America". America does not need transformed. It needs reminded that it has lost its way, but that it is not too late to restore honor, dignity, compassion, and decency to our Government. The real revolution occurs only from the bottom up in America. Armed with the tools presented here, perhaps you now have one more weapon in the arsenal to fight for America the way it should be. Now you know how they operate, and you will recognize their tactics when you see them.

The rest is up to you.

# ABOUT THE AUTHOR

Jeff Hedgpeth can be found online at:

http://www.AlinskyDefeater.com/Blog

https://twitter.com/AlinskyDefeater

http://www.facebook.com/AlinskyDefeaterFriendPage

http://www.facebook.com/pages/AlinskyDefeater/119243
588126065

## Notes

### Chapter 1

1  Clinton, Hillary. "There Is Only the Fight." *Gopublius.com*. N.p., n.d. Web. 1 May 2012.
<http://www.gopublius.com/HCT/HillaryClintonThesis.html>.

2  "Saul Alinsky." *DiscoverTheNetworks.org*. N.p., n.d. Web. 1 May 2012.
<http://www.discoverthenetworks.org/individualProfile.asp?in did=2314>.

3  Sanford D. Horwitt, *Let Them Call Me Rebel,* (New York: Random House, 1989), pp. 18-46

4  Saul Alinsky, Rules for Radicals (Toronto: Vintage Books, 1971), p. 4.

5  Saul Alinsky, *Rules for Radicals*, p. 7.

6  "Selected Quotations from the Thomas Jefferson Papers." *Library Of Congress*. N.p., n.d. Web. 1 May 2012.
<http://memory.loc.gov/ammem/collections/jefferson_papers/mtjquote.html>.

7  Ferrara, Peter. "Gingrich Frames the Debate." *The American Spectator*. N.p., 25 Jan. 2012. Web. 30 Apr. 2012.
<http://spectator.org/archives/2012/01/25/gingrich-frames-the-debate>.

8  Lizza, Ryan. "Saul Alinsky: a GOP Bogeyman Who Influences Many on the Left and Right." *Huffington Post*. N.p., 27 Jan. 2012. Web. 14 Apr. 2012.
<http://www.huffingtonpost.com/2012/01/27/saul-alinsky-newt-gingrich-obama_n_1236581.html>.

9  Lizza, Ryan. "The Agitator Barack Obama's Unlikely Political Education." *The New Republic*. N.p., 19 Mar. 2007. Web. 25 Apr. 2012. <http://www.tnr.com//article/the-agitator-barack-obamas-unlikely-political-education>.

10  "Obama, in His Own Words." *Fox News*. N.p., 22 Sept. 2009. Web. 1 May 2012.

<http://www.foxnews.com/story/0,2933,553880,00.html#ixzz1
rrHcJLjl>.

[11]   Saul Alinsky, *Rules for Radicals*, p. 103

[12]   "Carney: Obama's Community Organizer Experience
Contributed to Who He Is Today." *Real Clear Politics*. N.p., 23
Jan. 2012. Web. 1 May 2012.
<http://www.realclearpolitics.com/video/2012/01/23/carney_o
bamas_community_organizer_experience_contributed_to_who
_he_is_today.html>.

[13]   Barack Obama, *Dreams from My Father: A Story of Race
and Inheritance*. (New York: Times Books, 1995), pp. 99-100.

[14]   "CNN Turns Blind Eye to Obama-Alinsky Ties."
*Investors.com*. N.p., 26 Jan. 2012. Web. 1 May 2012.
<http://news.investors.com/article/599154/201201261854/me
dia-ignores-obama-alinsky-rules-for-radicals.htm>.

[15]   "Transcript: Michelle Obama's Convention Speech." *NPR*.
N.p., 25 Aug. 2008. Web. 1 May 2012.
<http://www.npr.org/templates/story/story.php?storyId=9396
3863>.

[16]   Saul Alinsky, *Rules for Radicals*, p. 3.

[17]   Saul Alinsky, *Rules for Radicals*, p. 12.

[18]   "What Is the Connection Between Obama and Saul Alinsky?
Read More: Http://www.foxnews.com/on-
air/oreilly/2012/01/25/what-connection-between-obama-and-
saul-alinsky#ixzz1tpdTJgFw." *Fox News*. N.p., 24 Jan. 2012.
Web. 1 May 2012. <http://www.foxnews.com/on-
air/oreilly/2012/01/25/what-connection-between-obama-and-
saul-alinsky>.

[19]   Alinsky, L. D. "Son Sees Father's Handiwork in Convention."
*BostonGlobe.com*. N.p., 31 Aug. 2008. Web. 1 May 2012.
<http://www.boston.com/bostonglobe/editorial_opinion/letter
s/articles/2008/08/31/son_sees_fathers_handiwork_in_conven
tion/>.

[20]   Saul Alinsky, *Rules for Radicals*, p.xxiii.

[21]  Saul Alinsky, *Rules for Radicals*, p. 18.

[22]  "The Declaration of Independence." *USHistory.org*. N.p., n.d. Web. 1 May 2012.
<http://www.ushistory.org/declaration/document/>.

[23]  "America Is a Shining City upon a Hill." *SourceWatch.org*. N.p., n.d. Web. 1 May 2012.
<http://www.sourcewatch.org/index.php?title=America_is_a_shining_city_upon_a_hill>.

[24]  "America's Place in the World Could Play Part in 2012 Elections." *USAToday.com*. N.p., 20 Jan. 2010. Web. 1 May 2012. <http://www.usatoday.com/news/washington/2010-12-21-1Aexceptional21_CV_N.htm>.

## Chapter 2

[1]  Sanford D. Horwitt, *Let Them Call Me Rebel*, p. 145 – 155.

[2]  Alinsky, Saul D. *Reveille for Radicals.* Toronto: Vintage Books, 1989. Reprint.

[3]  Raymond, Kim. "Consequentialism." *KimRaymond.com*. N.p., n.d. Web. 1 May 2012.
<http://kimraymond.com/kimraymond.com/Consequentialism.html>.

[4]  Saul Alinsky, *Rules for Radicals*, p. 24.

[5]  Saul Alinsky, *Rules for Radicals*, p. 26.

[6]  Saul Alinsky, *Rules for Radicals*, p. 3.

[7]  Saul Alinsky, *Rules for Radicals*, p. 15.

[8]  Saul Alinsky, *Rules for Radicals*, p. 17.

[9]  "Dualism." *Wikipedia.com*. N.p., n.d. Web. 1 May 2012.
<http://en.wikipedia.org/wiki/Dualism>.

[10]  Saul Alinsky, *Rules for Radicals*, p. 17 - 18.

[11]  Saul Alinsky, *Rules for Radicals*, p. 26.

[12]  Saul Alinsky, *Rules for Radicals*, p. 29.

[13]  Saul Alinsky, *Rules for Radicals*, p. 33.

[14]  Saul Alinsky, *Rules for Radicals*, p. 34.

15    "Geneva Conventions on the Protection of Victims of War." *ENotes.com*. N.p., n.d. Web. 1 May 2012. <http://www.enotes.com/topic/Geneva_Conventions>.

16    Saul Alinsky, *Rules for Radicals*, p. 37.

17    Saul Alinsky, *Rules for Radicals*, p. 45.

18    Sanford D. Horwitt, *Let Them Call Me Rebel*.

## Chapter 3

19    Saul Alinsky, *Rules for Radicals*, p. 3.

20    Saul Alinsky, *Rules for Radicals*, p. 67.

21    Saul Alinsky, *Rules for Radicals*, p. 139.

22    Saul Alinsky, *Rules for Radicals*, p. 137.

23    Saul Alinsky, *Rules for Radicals*, p. 117.

24    "Studs Terkel Interviews Saul Alinsky." N.p., n.d. Web. 1 May 2012. <http://www.youtube.com/watch?v=UrZ_mVdhzZ0>.

25    Saul Alinsky, *Rules for Radicals*, p. 116.

26    Saul Alinsky, *Rules for Radicals*, p. 126.

27    Lancel, Serge. *Hannibal.* (New Jersey: Blackwell Publishers, 1999).

28    Saul Alinsky, *Rules for Radicals*, p. 126.

29    Saul Alinsky, *Rules for Radicals*, p. 126.

30    Saul Alinsky, *Rules for Radicals*, p. 139.

31    Obama Declares White House Candidacy. Available at: http://archive.newsmax.com/archives/articles/2007/2/10/113431.shtml?s=tn [Accessed September 18, 2009].

32    "Another Report of Improper Obama Caucus Tactics." *TalkLeft.com*. N.p., 12 Mar. 2008. Web. 14 Nov. 2008. <http://www.talkleft.com/story/2008/3/12/155450/725>.

33    "Another Report of Improper Obama Caucus Tactics." *TalkLeft.com*. N.p., 12 Mar. 2008. Web. 14 Nov. 2008. <http://www.talkleft.com/story/2008/3/12/155450/725>.

[34]    Elving, Ron. "Caucus Strategy Bolsters Obama's Bid for White House." *NPR.org*. N.p., 12 Feb. 2008. Web. 21 Sept. 2009. <http://www.npr.org/blogs/watchingwashington/2008/02/caucus_strategy_bolsters_obama_1.html>.

[35]    Saul Alinsky, *Rules for Radicals*, p. 126.

[36]    Saul Alinsky, *Rules for Radicals*, p. 127.

[37]    Saul Alinsky, *Rules for Radicals*, p. 85 - 86.

[38]    AllahPundit. "Obama: McCain's Message Is That I Don't "look like the Other Presidents on the Currency"." *HotAir.com*. N.p., 30 July 2008. Web. 11 Oct. 2009. <http://hotair.com/archives/2008/07/30/obama-mccains-message-is-that-i-dont-look-like-the-other-presidents-on-the-currency/>.

[39]    Morrissey, Ed. "Who's Playing the Race Card? Update: Audio Added." *HotAir.com*. Http://hotair.com/archives/2008/06/21/whos-playing-the-race-card/, 21 June 2008. Web. 11 Oct. 2009.

[40]    Saul Alinsky, *Rules for Radicals*, p. 128.

[41]    Saul Alinsky, *Rules for Radicals*, p. 88.

[42]    "I Still Hate You, Sarah Palin - the Republicans Bring a Knife to a Gunfight, and Lose Again." *NationalReview.com*. N.p., 7 July 2009. Web. 28 Oct. 2009. <http://www.nationalreview.com/articles/227836/i-still-hate-you-sarah-palin/david-kahane>.

[43]    Ohlemacher, Stephen. "Obama Used Party Rules to Foil Clinton." *FreeRepublic.com*. N.p., 30 May 2008. Web. 17 Oct. 2009. <http://www.freerepublic.com/focus/f-news/2023407/posts>.

[44]    "Obama Ties McCain to Bush's Economic Policies." *CNN.com*. N.p., 20 Aug. 2008. Web. 17 Oct. 2009. <http://articles.cnn.com/2008-08-20/politics/campaign.wrap_1_obama-campaign-john-mccain-economic-plan?_s=PM:POLITICS>.

[45]    Saul Alinsky, *Rules for Radicals*, p. 128.

[46]    "Ridicule." *Dictionary.com*. N.p., n.d. Web. 1 May 2012. <http://dictionary.reference.com/browse/ridicule?s=t>.

[47]    Saul Alinsky, *Rules for Radicals*, p. 137 - 138.

48    "Obama, Saul Alinsky, Lucifer, Community Organizer, Ridicule, Socialists, McCain, Raila Odinga, ODM, Rules for Radicals, Alinsky Method, Ridicule Older People." N.p., 23 Dec. 2008. Web. 22 Oct. 2009. <http://citizenwells.wordpress.com/2008/09/23/obama-saul-alinsky-lucifer-community-organizer-ridicule-socialists-mccain-raila-odinga-odm-rules-for-radicals-alinsky-method-ridicule-older-people/>.

49    ""Still" Ad." *YouTube.com*. N.p., n.d. Web. 21 Oct. 2009. <http://www.youtube.com/watch?v=bQ2I0t_Twk0>.

50    "Why Doesn't McCain Use a Computer?" *ABCNews.go.com*. N.p., 14 Sept. 2008. Web. 14 Nov. 2009. <http://abcnews.go.com/blogs/politics/2008/09/why-doesnt-mcca/>.

51    Siegler, MG. "President Obama Admits That He's Never Used Twitter, but Thinks the Chinese Should Be Able To." *TechCrunch.com*. N.p., 15 Nov. 2009. Web. 1 May 2012. <http://techcrunch.com/2009/11/15/president-obama-twitter/>.

52    Knoller, Mark. "Obama Casts Republicans as Slurpee Sippers." *Cbsnews.com*. N.p., 8 Oct. 2010. Web. 1 May 2012. <http://www.cbsnews.com/8301-503544_162-20019115-503544.html>.

53    Portnoy, Howard. "Barack Obama's Sneer Campaign." *HotAir.com*. N.p., 18 Mar. 2012. Web. 1 May 2012. <http://hotair.com/greenroom/archives/2012/03/18/barack-obamas-sneer-campaign/>.

54    Sanford D. Horwitt, *Let Them Call Me Rebel,* p. 101.

55    Saul Alinsky, *Rules for Radicals*, p. 128.

56    Saul Alinsky, *Rules for Radicals*, p. 128.

57    Saul Alinsky, *Rules for Radicals*, p. 128.

58    Saul Alinsky, *Rules for Radicals*, p. 128.

59    Sanford D. Horwitt, *Let Them Call Me Rebel,* p. 39.

60    Marx, Karl, and Frederick Engels. "The Communist Manifesto." *Anu.edu*. N.p., n.d. Web. 1 May 2012. <http://www.anu.edu.au/polsci/marx/classics/manifesto.html>.

[61]   Saul Alinsky, *Rules for Radicals*, p. 139.

[62]   Malkin, Michelle. "Little Girl at Obama Town Hall Has Not-so-random Political Connections." *Michellemalkin.com*. N.p., 11 Aug. 2009. Web. 1 May 2012.
<http://michellemalkin.com/2009/08/11/little-girl-at-obama-town-hall-has-not-so-random-political-connections/>.

[63]   Saul Alinsky, *Rules for Radicals*, p. 61.

[64]   Saul Alinsky, *Rules for Radicals*, p. 67.

[65]   Saul Alinsky, *Rules for Radicals*, p. 140.

[66]   Saul Alinsky, *Rules for Radicals*, p. 138.

[67]   Seib, Gerald F. "In Crisis, Opportunity for Obama." *WallStreetJournal.com*. N.p., 21 Nov. 2008. Web. 1 May 2012.
<http://online.wsj.com/article/SB122721278056345271.html>.

[68]   Saul Alinsky, *Rules for Radicals*, p. 129.

[69]   Saul Alinsky, *Rules for Radicals*, pp. 146 - 147.

[70]   Horowitz, David. "ACORN, Obama Behind Plan to Dump Garbage on Speaker Boehner's Home?" *FreeRepublic.com*. N.p., 9 Apr. 2011. Web. 1 May 2012.
<http://www.freerepublic.com/focus/f-chat/2702259/posts>.

[71]   Saul Alinsky, *Rules for Radicals*, p. 129.

[72]   "Obama Takes a Page from Alinsky Handbook." *Letfreedomringusa.com*. N.p., 7 Sept. 2009. Web. 1 May 2012.
<http://www.letfreedomringusa.com/news/read/657>.

[73]   Saul Alinsky, *Rules for Radicals*, p. 159.

[74]   Saul Alinsky, *Rules for Radicals*, p. 130.

[75]   Saul Alinsky, *Rules for Radicals*, p. 132.

[76]   Saul Alinsky, *Rules for Radicals*, p. 130.

[77]   Saul Alinsky, *Rules for Radicals*, p. 134.

## Chapter 4

[1]   "1984 There You Go Again...again." *PBS.org*. N.p., n.d. Web. 1 May 2012.

<http://www.pbs.org/newshour/debatingourdestiny/dod/1984
-broadcast.html>.
2   Saul Alinsky, *Rules for Radicals*, p. 129.

## Chapter 5

1   "Transcript: Illinois Senate Candidate Barack Obama."
*WashingtonPost.com*. N.p., 27 July 2004. Web. 1 May 2012.
<http://www.washingtonpost.com/wp-dyn/articles/A19751-
2004Jul27.html>.
2   "Biden Calls Paying Higher Taxes a Patriotic Act."
*MSNBC.com*. N.p., 18 Sept. 2008. Web. 1 May 2012.
<http://www.msnbc.msn.com/id/26771716/ns/politics-
decision_08/t/biden-calls-paying-higher-taxes-patriotic-act/>.
3   Weigel, David. "Tea Party Infiltration Done Wrong."
*Slate.com*. N.p., 9 Aug. 2010. Web. 1 May 2012.
<http://www.slate.com/content/slate/blogs/weigel/2010/08/0
9/tea_party_infiltration_done_wrong.html>.
4   Schilling, Chelsea. "Town Halls Burst with Obama 'plants'."
*WND.com*. N.p., 13 Aug. 2009. Web. 1 May 2012.
<http://www.wnd.com/2009/08/106811/>.
5   Huston, Warner T. "Dem. Shill as 'Attendee' in Obama
Healthcare Townhall -- Where's Media Finger-wagging?"
*NewsBusters.org*. N.p., 15 June 2010. Web. 1 May 2012.
<http://newsbusters.org/blogs/warner-todd-
huston/2009/06/15/shill-attendee-obamas-healthcare-
townhall-audience-wheres-media->.
6   Sanford D. Horwitt, *Let Them Call Me Rebel*.
7   Sanford D. Horwitt, *Let Them Call Me Rebel*, p. 60.
8   Shear, Michael D. "Obama Releases Long-Form Birth
Certificate." *Http://thecaucus.blogs.nytimes.com*. N.p., 27 Apr.
2011. Web. 1 May 2012.

<http://thecaucus.blogs.nytimes.com/2011/04/27/obamas-long-form-birth-certificate-released/>.

[9]    "Memorandum." N.p., n.d. Web. 1 May 2012.
<http://i2.cdn.turner.com/cnn/2010/images/01/26/managersmemojan.pdf>.

[10]    Saul Alinsky, *Rules for Radicals*, p. xxiii.

[11]    Saul Alinsky, *Rules for Radicals*, p. 103.

76402579R00115

Made in the USA
San Bernardino, CA
11 May 2018